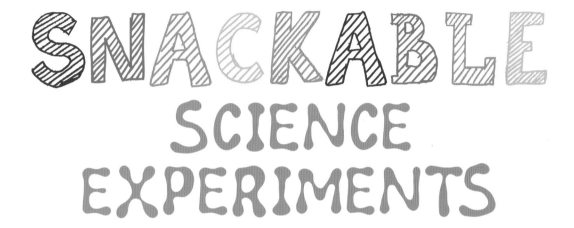

SNACKABLE SCIENCE EXPERIMENTS

60 EDIBLE TESTS TO TRY AND TASTE

EMMA VANSTONE

Author of *This Is Rocket Science*

PAGE STREET
PUBLISHING CO.

PAGE STREET
PUBLISHING CO.

First published in 2019 by

Page Street Publishing Co.

27 Congress Street, Suite 105

Salem, MA 01970

www.pagestreetpublishing.com

Distributed by Macmillan, sales in Canada by The Canadian Manda Group.

23   22   21   20   19   1   2   3   4   5

ISBN-13: 978-1-62414-822-4

ISBN-10: 1-62414-822-0

Library of Congress Control Number: 2018962651

Cover and book design by Kylie Alexander for Page Street Publishing Co.

Photography by Charlotte Dart

Printed and bound in China

FOR ZAK, SYDNEY, HANNAH
AND CHARLIE

CONTENTS

INTRODUCTION

Do you know why pretzels are a dark-brown color, why honeycomb is full of bubbles or how to remove the shell of an egg without touching it? Investigate your way around the kitchen with this fun collection of sixty snackable science experiments. You could even make a three-course meal from the investigations. How about homemade breadsticks and guacamole (made from avocados ripened using some science trickery) to start, followed by a choice of thick- or thin-crust pizza with a beautiful Baked Alaska to finish? Serve the meal with special homemade lemonade that gets its fizz from using the power of baking soda, and add some sinking and floating lemons to garnish. Did you realize there was so much science in your kitchen?

The great thing about science in the kitchen is that you probably already have everything you need for most of the experiments in this book—and you can eat the result! Warm up in winter with a magical hot chocolate and cool down in summer with a rainbow slushy drink made using the freezing power of salt and ice. Make fruity gummy sweets for your friends and discover which ingredients make their favorite type of cookie! The learning opportunities in the kitchen are endless and are a great way to spend time with friends or family. I've spent many, many happy afternoons chatting with my children as we've experimented with different ingredients and ideas.

Have a look through this book, then create, bake and learn all at the same time. You'll soon be making your own baking soda, testing the pH of lemon juice, extracting the color from candy and making models of DNA, cells and soil layers.

The activities in this book are all independent of one another, so don't feel you need to do them in order. And remember that science experiments don't work perfectly all the time, but there's always a reason why—even when it all goes wrong, there's still a lot to learn. Each activity in this book has been thoroughly tested by my little testing team and found to be tasty enough to include. Every experiment in this book is exciting, educational and, most of all, fun!

Emma Vanstone

INVESTIGATE

Investigate your way around the kitchen with these exciting and almost entirely edible experiments. Make your own pH indicator from red cabbage, create magical mixtures, discover which colors are hiding in your candy and remove the shell from an egg without boiling it first.

Invite your friends for a pizza-cheese testing party, but don't forget to make sure the avocados for the guacamole are ripe beforehand with our special science trick. You could even send them home with a homemade hot chocolate stick so they can watch the chocolate swirl around the milk as it melts.

Remember to make sure you set up each experiment as a fair test. This means keeping everything the same except the variable you want to test. For example, use the same amount of milk and hot chocolate powder before making Magical Mixtures on page 14 (the variable here is the temperature of the milk) and the same amount of each test cheese on your pizzas in the Cheesy Pizza experiment on page 25 (the variable here is the type of cheese). This helps keep your investigation as fair as possible.

COLOR-CHANGING PAPER

Acids and alkalis are substances that can be found in the science laboratory and in the home. Very strong acids and alkalis can be dangerous, but weak acids and alkalis are found in everyday things such as lemon juice (an acid) and bicarbonate of soda (an alkali).

An indicator is a substance that changes color when added to an acidic or an alkaline solution. Red cabbage contains a pigment called anthocyanin—this is a pigment that changes color depending on the pH of its environment, making it a brilliant pH indicator.

You can make your own indicator very easily using just red cabbage and water. To make indicator paper, simply dip filter paper into red-cabbage water and leave it to dry.

INGREDIENTS

Coarsely chopped red cabbage

Water

Vinegar

Lemon juice

Baking soda

SUPPLIES

Small pot

Sieve

Medium bowl

White coffee filter or scientific filter paper

Scissors

Plate or tray

4 small containers

Pipette or dropper

Place the red cabbage in a small pot. Cover the cabbage with cold water and bring it to a boil over medium heat.

Reduce the heat to low and let the red cabbage simmer for about 10 minutes, or until the water turns a deep purple color.

Remove the pot from the heat and let the cabbage and water cool.

Once the cabbage and water are cool, carefully pour the cabbage water through a sieve into a medium bowl. This is your red-cabbage indicator.

You don't need the cabbage anymore, but you can eat it.

Carefully cut your filter paper into strips with scissors. The strips should be about ⅜ x 4 inches (1 x 10 cm).

Dip each strip of filter paper, one at a time, into the red-cabbage water so it's completely wet. Leave the strips to dry on a plate. Keep the spare red-cabbage liquid (indicator liquid) safe.

(continued)

COLOR-CHANGING PAPER (CONT.)

Once they are dry, your indicator strips are ready to use.

Put a small amount of vinegar in the first small container, the lemon juice in the second container, 1 teaspoon of baking soda and water in the third container and plain water in the fourth container.

Carefully use the pipette to drop a small amount of each test liquid onto an indicator strip. The strip should change color, depending on the substance you test.

The red-cabbage indicator paper turns red or pink if dipped into an acidic solution and green if dipped in an alkaline solution.

MORE FUN

- Try testing lemonade, milk, soda water and lime juice. Can you guess what color the indicator paper will turn for each liquid?
- Did you know acids and bases react together? This is called a neutralization reaction. Put a little baking soda in a beaker and add vinegar or lemon juice, and watch what happens!
- For a colorful reaction, pour a little red-cabbage indicator into a beaker, add 1 teaspoon of baking soda, mix well and then add vinegar—you should find the mixture changes color and fizzes.

LEARNING POINTS

- The actual shade of color will depend on the strength of the acid or alkali. If there is no color change, the substance is neutral.

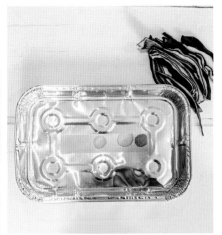

A mixture is made when at least two different substances are combined. Mixtures can be easily separated, with the substances in the mixture keeping their original properties.

Imagine mixing cereal and marshmallows—it would make a tasty breakfast mixture, but the individual components (cereal and marshmallows) could easily be separated using a filter.

MAGICAL MIXTURES

A solution is a mixture where one substance dissolves in another. For example, if you add sugar to a cup of tea, the sugar dissolves in the tea, giving you a solution of tea and sugar.

This experiment investigates whether the temperature of milk (the solution) affects how easily hot chocolate powder dissolves.

INGREDIENTS

Water

Hot chocolate powder

Sugar

Sand

Hot milk

Cold milk

Chocolate buttons or grated chocolate

SUPPLIES

Up to 8 cups or beakers (depending on whether or not you wash and reuse them)

Teaspoon

Take 3 cups and fill each one halfway with cold water. Add 1 teaspoon of one test substance to each cup: hot chocolate powder in the first cup, sugar in the second cup and sand in the third cup.

Stir each mixture for 30 seconds.

Try this process again, but this time, use warm water. Does more of the test substance dissolve?

Now try to dissolve hot chocolate powder in hot and cold milk. Fill one cup with hot milk and one with cold milk. Add 2 teaspoons (4 g) of hot chocolate powder to each cup and stir for 30 seconds.

You should find hot chocolate powder doesn't dissolve very much in cold milk, but when it is added to hot milk, you end up with a lovely, smooth hot chocolate!

Try this process again, but this time use chocolate buttons. You should find that the chocolate buttons dissolve in the hot milk, but not the cold milk.

(continued)

Adult Supervision

MAGICAL MIXTURES (CONT.)

MORE FUN

- Two things that affect the speed at which a solid dissolves are the temperature and the size of the grains of the solid.

- Solids dissolve faster in hot water, as hot water molecules are moving faster—they bump into the solid more often, which increases the rate of the reaction.

- You can test this using sugar cubes and grains of sugar. Try the investigation again, but this time add sugar grains to one cup of hot water and the same amount of sugar cubes to another cup of hot water. Does one dissolve faster than the other?

- Try mixing liquids. Juice and water mix together easily, but oil and water do not mix. (Hint: Try adding a little dish soap to the oil and water; this should allow them to mix, as dish soap is an emulsifier, meaning that it holds the oil and water together.)

LEARNING POINTS

- We call substances that dissolve in a liquid *soluble*. Sugar and salt are examples of soluble substances. Sand is insoluble, because it doesn't dissolve in water.

- Grains of sugar dissolve faster than a sugar cube, as more surface area of the sugar is in contact with the water, which also makes the reaction happen faster.

Carefully add the chocolate powder.

Stir!

Does the chocolate powder dissolve?

HIDDEN CANDY COLORS

Did you know that some food colors (and inks) are made up of more than one color? The colors can be separated using a technique called chromatography.

Chromatography is a technique used to separate mixtures. The mixture is passed through another substance, in this case filter paper, to separate the components. The different color particles travel at different speeds through the filter paper, allowing you to see the different colors each mixture is made from.

INGREDIENTS

M&M's®, Skittles or other colored candy

SUPPLIES

Plate or tray

Pipettes

Water

Filter paper, cut into strips

Place the M&M's on a plate.

Carefully use a pipette to drip a few drops of water onto each candy piece and let the candy soak until the water has turned the same color as the candy. Color from each candy piece will dissolve into the water.

Use a pipette to suck up the colored water from each candy piece one by one and carefully drip the water onto the bottom of a strip of filter paper. Use a separate strip of filter paper and a clean pipette for each color.

Leave the filter paper strips on a plate for about 10 minutes and observe what happens.

You should find that different color bands appear on the filter paper strips. This is because the coloring on the candy shells is a mixture of colors that have separated out.

MORE FUN

• Try the same technique with a different type of candy. Do all green candies give the same color pattern?

• You can also try this with felt-tip pens. Instead of dropping color from a candy onto the filter paper, draw a circle on the filter paper using a colored pen and use a pipette to drip a few drops of water over the circle.

LEARNING POINTS

• The candy colors separate because, as the water moves up the filter paper, it carries the color mixture with it.

• Different components of the color mixture move at different rates, meaning the colors can be seen separately on the filter paper.

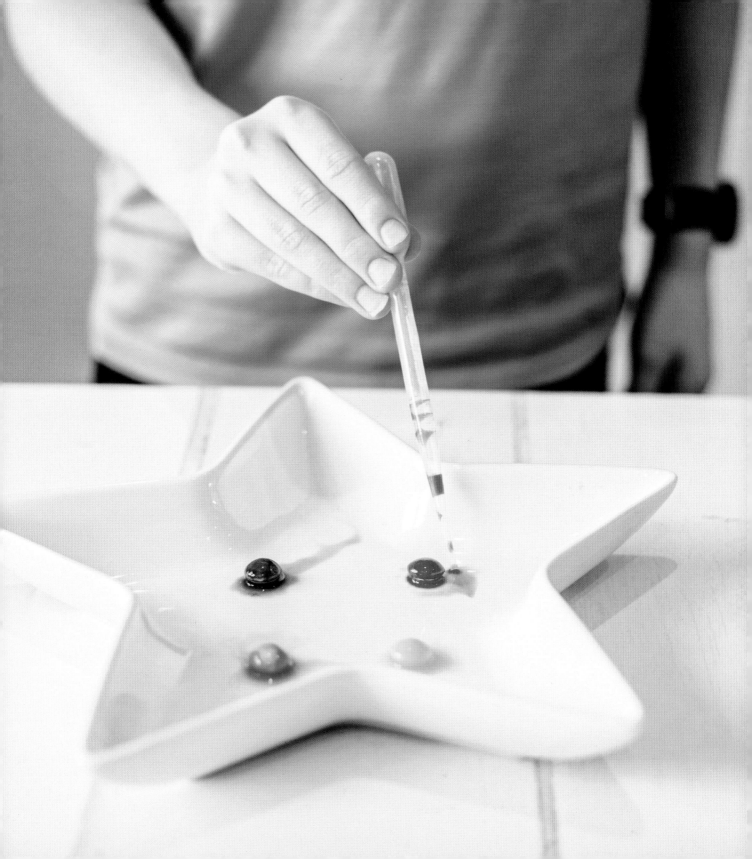

BUBBLY HONEYCOMB

Have you ever wondered why honeycomb has lots of bubbles? We're going to find out!

A key ingredient when making honeycomb is golden syrup. This is an amber-colored, sweet syrup that has been inverted. This means the sucrose (what we think of as sugar) has been broken down into two simpler sugars: fructose and glucose. It is the golden syrup that gives honeycomb its distinctive color, and the addition of baking soda makes the mixture bubble.

INGREDIENTS

Butter (or foil or parchment paper)

½ cup (100 g) superfine (caster) sugar

1 tbsp (15 ml) water

2 tbsp (30 ml) golden syrup

1 tsp baking soda

Melted chocolate (optional)

SUPPLIES

Medium baking pan

Medium pot

Wooden spoon or spatula

Candy thermometer (optional)

Grease a medium baking pan with a small amount of butter or line it with foil or parchment paper.

Carefully pour the superfine (caster) sugar, water and golden syrup into a medium pot over low heat. Stir for a few minutes with a wooden spoon or spatula, until the sugar has completely melted. You shouldn't be able to feel any grains of sugar at the bottom of the saucepan at this stage.

Increase the heat to medium and bring the mixture to a boil until it is caramel colored. This will take about 5 minutes. If you have a candy thermometer, the mixture should be around 300°F (150°C).

Quickly turn off the heat and add the baking soda, gently folding it into the sugar mixture with a wooden spoon. The mixture will froth up.

Carefully pour the mixture into the prepared baking pan and leave it to cool.

Once the honeycomb has set, you can carefully snap it into pieces.

To make the honeycomb extra special, drizzle melted chocolate over the top, if desired.

MORE FUN

- What happens if you add twice the amount of baking soda?
- Heating the sugar mixture to 300°F (150°C) makes the honeycomb hard and brittle. If you prefer your honeycomb chewier, heat it to around 265°F (130°C).

LEARNING POINTS

- The heat of the sugar mixture breaks down the baking soda, releasing carbon dioxide gas, which makes the mixture froth up. The bubbles from the carbon dioxide stay in the mixture as it sets.

FRESHLY FILTERED APPLE CIDER

Apple cider is delicious served warm in winter or chilled over ice in summer. You can tweak the recipe to your own taste, experiment with different types of apples and maybe even add an orange or two.

Apple cider is raw apple juice, which has usually not been pasteurized or filtered to remove all the apple sediment. Apple juice is different than cider, as it is usually filtered to remove all solids and pasteurized so it stays fresh longer.

Making apple cider at home is a great way to learn about filtering.

INGREDIENTS

8 apples
2 cinnamon sticks
1 tsp ground allspice

SUPPLIES

Knife
Large pot
Water
Masher
Wooden spoon
Sieve
Large jug
Cheesecloth

Carefully chop each apple into quarters with a knife. Place the apple quarters in a large pot and cover the apples with water.

Simmer the apples for about 1 hour over low heat. Mash the apples and add the cinnamon sticks and allspice. Stir the mixture with a wooden spoon, cover the pot and simmer for another 2 hours.

Strain the mixture through a sieve into a large jug. Discard the apple bits left in the sieve, line the sieve with a cheesecloth and strain the cider again.

You should find the apple cider looks less cloudy after being passed through the sieve and less cloudy again after passing through the cheesecloth.

Apple cider can be drunk warm or chilled from the fridge.

MORE FUN

- Try adding ½ cup (72 g) of brown sugar to the recipe. How do you think this will affect the taste?
- Can you smell the cinnamon and allspice? What other spices would be good to add? How about cloves?

LEARNING POINTS

- Filtration is one way to separate solids from a liquid. When the apple cider mixture is filtered, the solid apple pieces are left behind in the sieve. The juice is filtered twice to remove the larger pieces and then the smaller apple sediment. The holes in the cheesecloth are much smaller than the holes in the sieve, so the second filtering stage removes smaller pieces of apple residue than the first.

Adult Supervision

CHEESY PIZZA

How do you like your pizza cheese? Do you find the stretching of cheese as you pull a slice satisfying, or would you rather have a clean cut with no stringy bits? Do you like pizza cheese brown and bubbly or pale and chewy? In this activity, you're going to test different types of cheeses to discover which you prefer and find out how they are different.

Mozzarella is commonly used on pizzas, as it has a high water content and melts well with a stringy texture. Cheeses with a lower water content, such as cheddar, don't melt as well and aren't as stretchy.

INGREDIENTS

Pizza dough (store-bought or homemade [page 34])

Tomato pizza topping

4 cheeses to test (such as mozzarella, cheddar, provolone, Parmesan, Gouda, Edam)

SUPPLIES

Baking sheet

Spoon

Pizza cutter

Preheat the oven to 355°F (180°C).

Place the pizza dough on a baking sheet. Spread the tomato pizza sauce evenly over the pizza dough with a spoon.

Divide the pizza into quarters and place a different type of cheese on each quarter. Try to make sure the cheese segments are the same size and thickness to make it a fair test.

Bake the pizza in the oven for 10 to 12 minutes, or until the cheeses start to brown.

How does each type of cheese look? Have some melted better than others? Which have browned the most?

Leave the pizza to cool for a few minutes and then ask an adult to help cut it into slices with a pizza cutter. Make sure you cut down the center of each quarter along the cheeses so you have 8 slices.

Separate the pizza slices. How does the cheese on each slice stretch?

Taste a slice from each quarter of the pizza. Can you tell the difference between the cheeses? Which do you like the best?

MORE FUN

- Add some toppings to the pizza with half under the cheese and half over the cheese. Does this affect how the cheese melts and looks?
- Make a pizza using half low-fat mozzarella and half full-fat. You should find the cheese with the higher fat content melts better.

LEARNING POINTS

- Cheese is made up mostly of protein, fat and water. The cheese is held together by a mesh of proteins, with fat and water trapped inside. The more fat and water a cheese has, the softer the cheese.

HOT CHOCOLATE STICKS

Hot chocolate sticks are easy to make, are a great way to learn about changes of state and also make a lovely gift.

The chocolate starts off as a solid, melts when heated in the microwave, becomes solid again as it cools in the mold and then melts again when it is put into hot milk to make delicious hot chocolate!

Chocolate melts around 85°F (30°C), which is lower than body temperature and explains why chocolate melts in your mouth.

INGREDIENTS

6¾ oz (200 g) chocolate

Mug of hot milk

Decorations (such as fudge, marshmallows, candy cane pieces and sprinkles; optional)

SUPPLIES

Medium bowl

Wooden spoon or spatula

Silicone candy mold

Lollipop sticks

Break the chocolate into small pieces and place them in a medium bowl. Heat the chocolate carefully in a microwave in 20-second intervals, stirring after each interval with a wooden spoon or spatula, until the chocolate is fully melted.

Once the chocolate is melted, carefully pour the chocolate into the candy mold, place a lollipop stick in the chocolate and place the mold in the fridge until set.

To make hot chocolate, stir the hot chocolate stick into the mug of hot milk until it melts.

MORE FUN

• Add decorations to the hot chocolate stick by placing them on top of the melted chocolate in the mold around the lollipop stick.

• Do these decorations melt completely? How do they change the taste of the hot chocolate?

LEARNING POINTS

• Everything exists as a solid, liquid or gas, but some substances can change state if heated or cooled. This means they can change from a liquid to a solid, a solid to a liquid or a liquid to a gas.

• Be careful not to let the chocolate come into contact with any water during the melting process, as water makes chocolate turn lumpy and grainy (which won't make a nice drink).

RIPEN AN AVOCADO

Avocados can be hard to buy at the perfect stage to eat. Too hard and they don't taste very pleasant, too soft and they start to discolor inside and lose their taste.

If you slice open an avocado and find it's not quite ready, put it back together, wrap it in cling film and leave it in the fridge for a few days. The perfect avocado should be soft but still slightly firm.

If there's no choice but to buy an avocado that's not quite ready, use this trick to speed up the ripening process.

INGREDIENTS

3 hard avocados
1 kiwi
1 banana

SUPPLIES

3 brown paper bags
Pen or pencil

Place 1 avocado in each of the brown paper bags. Label the bags 1, 2 and 3 with a pen.

Place a kiwi in bag 2 and a banana in bag 3. Roll down the top of each bag to seal it. Leave the bags out at room temperature.

Check the avocados each day, remembering to seal the bags after checking.

Record how many days it takes for the avocado in each bag to ripen.

MORE FUN

- This time try the experiment with 2 bananas or kiwis in the bags with the avocados. Do the avocados ripen faster?
- Test to see whether the same method works with unripe tomatoes.

LEARNING POINTS

- Avocados release ethylene gas slowly, which makes the fruit ripen. The paper bag traps the ethylene gas, making the avocado ripen faster. Bananas and kiwis also release ethylene gas, so when these are also trapped in a bag with an avocado, the increased level of ethylene gas should make the avocado ripen faster than when it is in a bag with no extra fruit.

REMOVE A SHELL WITHOUT TOUCHING IT

You've probably picked the shell off a hard-boiled egg, but did you know you can remove the shell from a fresh egg without touching it? All you need is vinegar!

This clever trick is sure to impress your friends. You can even gently squeeze the shell-less egg with your fingers or bounce it from a low height without it breaking.

INGREDIENTS

1 raw egg
Distilled white vinegar

SUPPLIES

Small container

Carefully place the egg in a small container and cover it with the vinegar. You should see bubbles appear after about 1 hour. These are bubbles of carbon dioxide, which is released as the shell reacts with the vinegar.

Leave the egg in the vinegar for about 24 hours, then carefully remove it from the container. You should be able to remove most of the shell by gently rubbing the egg.

Wash the egg carefully with cold water and cover it with fresh vinegar. After another 24 hours, you should be able to rub the rest of the shell away, leaving a naked egg.

Try gently squeezing the egg. Is the membrane stronger than you expected?

MORE FUN

- Can you bounce your naked egg? Try dropping it gently into a tray. You should find the egg bounces! How high can you bounce the egg before it breaks?
- Change the color of your egg by placing it in colored water—you should find the colored water passes through the egg membrane into the contents of the egg.
- Shrink your egg by placing it into a concentrated solution (such as corn syrup) for a few days. In this instance, water molecules will move from the egg into the concentrated solution to make the water concentration on both sides of the egg membrane the same.
- Place the egg in water to grow it again.

(continued)

REMOVE A SHELL WITHOUT TOUCHING IT (CONT.)

LEARNING POINTS

- The eggshell breaks down as acetic acid in vinegar reacts with the calcium carbonate and releases carbon dioxide gas, which can be seen as bubbles.

- You should find that the egg looks bigger than when you first started. This is because the membrane around the contents of the egg is semipermeable (which means water can pass through it), so water from the vinegar moves through the membrane to the inside of the egg. This movement of water molecules is called osmosis. Vinegar has a higher concentration of water than the inside of the egg, so water molecules move from the vinegar into the egg until the concentration of water is the same in the vinegar as in the egg.

Adult Supervision

PIZZA CRUSTS

How do you like your pizza dough? Thick and chewy or thin and crispy? Whatever your pizza preference, you can tweak the ingredients making up the dough to make it perfect just for you.

Thin-crust pizza has thinner, more delicate dough, which cooks quickly. It's best to limit the number of toppings on this kind of dough, as it can get soggy.

Thicker dough takes longer to cook but can tolerate more toppings, so if you like to load your pizza up, a thick dough is what you need.

THIN CRUST

⅓ cup (80 ml) lukewarm water

½ tsp instant yeast

½ tsp salt

1½ cups (150 g) bread flour

THICK CRUST

⅓ cup (80 ml) lukewarm water

1 tsp instant yeast

½ tbsp (6 g) superfine (caster) sugar

½ tsp salt

1½ cups (150 g) bread flour

SUPPLIES

2 large bowls

Rolling pin

Baking sheet

Pour the water into a large bowl and gently stir in the yeast, sugar (if making thick crust) and salt. Add the flour slowly and knead it with your hands. The mixture should start to bind together. The dough should become smooth and spongy but not sticky, so add more flour if you need it. If the dough is too dry, add a bit more water.

Lightly dust another large bowl with flour, place the dough in the bowl and leave it in a warm area until the dough has doubled in size.

Use a rolling pin to roll and stretch the dough out onto a baking sheet. If you are making a thick-crust pizza, the dough should be about ⅜-inch (1-cm) thick. If you are making a thin-crust pizza, the dough should be ³⁄₁₆-inch (0.5-cm) thick.

MORE FUN

- Did you know you can use the power of yeast to blow up a balloon? First, blow up the balloon and let the air out. Pour 1 teaspoon of yeast and 1 teaspoon of sugar into a small bottle. Fill the bottle halfway with lukewarm water, and quickly stretch the balloon's opening over the bottle's opening. Give the mixture a shake and you should find the balloon blows up, thanks to the carbon dioxide gas produced by the yeast.

LEARNING POINTS

- Yeast is a living single-celled organism commonly used in baking. Yeast is a type of leavener (baking soda and baking powder can also be used as leaveners).

- Yeast converts sugar and starch (from the sugar and flour) into carbon dioxide and alcohol. The carbon dioxide makes the dough rise. Yeast works best in a warm, moist environment, which is why you leave the dough somewhere warm to rise.

- Sugar is added to the thick-crust dough, as this increases the activity of the yeast. You should find the thick-crust dough grows in size more than the thin crust.

CREATE

Use the power of science to discover how to put ice cream in a hot oven without it melting, make a slushy drink without a freezer and then hold the freezing cold slushy drink without your hands getting cold.

Make your toast more exciting with some flavored butter, followed by a density ice lolly for any season.

Play and then eat edible Tetris and Jenga® games and be as creative with the decorating as you want. There's no limit to what you can create. Make the pieces plain or sparkly, cover them with chocolate or candy—the choice is yours.

NO MORE COLD HANDS

Have you ever held a snow cone and found it gets a little bit too cold to hold? This is because heat and cold like to travel. When you hold a snow cone, heat is traveling from your warm body to the cold treat, which makes it start to melt, and as your hand loses heat it starts to feel colder.

Your challenge in this activity is to create something that fits around the snow cone container to stop the cold from reaching your hands.

INGREDIENTS

Rainbow Fruit Slushies (page 42)

SUPPLIES

Snow cone holder or paper cup
Corrugated cardboard
Aluminum foil
Felt or cotton
Bubble Wrap
Tape

Wrap a snow cone holder in each of your test materials (corrugated cardboard, aluminum foil, felt and Bubble Wrap) and fix it in place with the tape.

Fill the snow cone holder with the Rainbow Fruit Slushy.

Feel each wrapped snow cone holder every 30 seconds for 5 minutes and record which feels cold first.

Use your findings to create a decorated insulating band that fits around the snow cone holder.

MORE FUN

• As heat from your hand can't reach the snow cone (thanks to the insulation), you should find the slush stays frozen for longer. Can you test this?

• An insulated flask can keep food or drinks hot or cold, as it has two walls with a vacuum (no air) between them. There's nothing in the flask to keep food hot or cold; rather, it doesn't allow heat (or cold) to escape. Heat and cold are transferred through air, but as there is no air, there is nothing to transfer the heat or cold. How long does your snow cone stay frozen in an insulated flask?

LEARNING POINTS

• An insulator is a material that doesn't allow heat or cold to pass through it.

• Bubble Wrap is a great insulator as it contains lots of small air bubbles. Air is a good insulator, as it doesn't let heat or cold pass through it easily.

• You should find that the aluminum foil doesn't protect your hands against the cold as it is a conductor, not an insulator. Conductors transfer heat and cold easily, which is useful in some situations, but not in this case!

FLAVORED BUTTER

Have you ever made some toast and then realized you didn't have any butter to go with it? If you have a jar and some cream, you can make your own!

Cream is a special type of mixture called a colloid. Colloids have tiny particles of one substance scattered through another substance. Cream is a colloid as it's made up of tiny particles of fat dispersed in water.

Shaking cream makes the fat droplets stick together, giving you butter.

INGREDIENTS

Heavy cream

Finely chopped fresh parsley (optional)

Lime zest (optional)

Honey (optional)

Ground cinnamon (optional)

Ground nutmeg or mixed spice (optional)

SUPPLIES

Jar with a lid

Sieve

Medium bowl

Rolling pin

Parchment paper

Take the cream out of the fridge and let it stand for about 30 minutes so it reaches room temperature.

Fill the jar about half full of cream.

Close the jar's lid tightly and shake the cream for about 10 minutes. After about 10 minutes, you should feel a lump in the jar along with the liquid. The liquid is buttermilk. Carefully pour the contents of the jar through the sieve over the medium bowl. Discard the buttermilk and transfer the solid back to the jar.

Shake the jar again for about 3 minutes and pour the buttery mixture through the sieve into the bowl again to remove the last of the buttermilk.

Holding the butter in your hands, rinse it under cold water. Knead it on a clean, dry surface to remove as much of the buttermilk as possible. Rinse the butter again—it is now ready to eat.

If desired, you can add one of the following: parsley, lime zest, honey, cinnamon or nutmeg. Adding flavor is optional but makes your butter extra special.

To add flavor to the butter, use a rolling pin to roll the butter out on a large sheet of parchment paper and add a thin layer of your chosen flavoring. Gently roll the butter into a sausage shape and slice.

Remember homemade butter won't keep for long, but will last 3 to 4 days if kept in the fridge.

MORE FUN

- Try making butter again, but this time stop shaking the jar before the lump of butter appears—you should see a whipped-cream stage first.

LEARNING POINTS

- A mixture is two or more substances mixed together but not chemically combined (they can be separated).
- Your homemade butter won't look or taste like the butter you buy from a store, as store-bought butter usually has extra ingredients added to it to make it taste better and look more attractive.

Adult Supervision

RAINBOW FRUIT SLUSHIES

Did you know you can make a slushy drink without a freezer or special machine? All you need is the special freezing power of salt and ice!

Pure water freezes at 32°F (0°C). Salt lowers the freezing temperature of water by a few degrees. If salt is added to ice, the ice is then above its freezing point and starts to melt, which requires energy. In this activity, heat energy required for the ice to melt is absorbed from the fruity drink, which makes tiny ice crystals form in the juice, giving you a lovely slushy mixture!

Remember, the ice and salt mixture will get very cold, so do not let it come into direct contact with your skin.

INGREDIENTS
1 cup (240 ml) fruity drink
Ice
2 tbsp (30 g) salt

SUPPLIES
2 large zip-top bags
Tea towel (optional)
Cup or bowl
Spoon

Pour the fruity drink into a zip-top bag and seal the bag carefully.

Fill the other zip-top bag halfway with ice and add the salt.

Place the bag containing the fruity drink into the bag of ice and give it a good shake.

Try to keep the fruity drink in contact with the ice as much as possible and roll the ice over the bag containing the fruity drink. The ice will start to feel much colder, so you might need to place a tea towel between the bag and your hands. Continue this process for 5 minutes.

Check the fruity drink after 5 minutes—it should be starting to turn to slush, but if not keep going until you feel the drink turn to slush.

Once you have a lovely slushy, pour it into a cup or bowl and eat it immediately with a spoon.

MORE FUN
- Experiment with flavored milks and different juices to find the best slushy ingredients.

LEARNING POINTS
- When salt is mixed with ice, it makes the ice melt as it lowers the freezing point of the ice—this is known as freezing-point depression. The more salt you add, the lower the freezing point.
- You should find the ice feels extra cold, which is why you'll need a towel to cover the bag after a few minutes.
- Salt is often spread onto roads during cold snaps, as salt makes the ice on the road melt even if the air temperature is cold enough for it to freeze.

BAKE ICE CREAM WITHOUT MELTING IT

How can you put ice cream in a hot oven without it melting? Cover it with meringue!

Baked Alaska looks amazing and a lot more complex than it actually is. The sponge cake, ice cream and fluffy meringue make a tasty pudding with a surprising feature. The secret to a good Baked Alaska is to cook it for long enough to bake the meringue but not long enough to melt the ice cream.

INGREDIENTS

Sponge cake

Jam

Vanilla ice cream

3 egg whites

¾ cup plus 1½ tbsp (175 g) superfine (caster) sugar

½ tsp cream of tartar

SUPPLIES

Knife

Medium baking sheet

Dariole molds, small bowls or pudding dishes

Cling film

Medium bowl

Whisk

MORE FUN

- Make your own ice cream using the fruity slush method on page 42.
- Experiment with different types of cake and ice cream to find your favorite combination.

Preheat the oven to 390°F (200°C).

Slice the cake so you have five ⅜-inch (1-cm) thick slices with a knife. Spread each with a layer of jam and place each on a medium baking sheet. Press the dariole mold or small bowl into the cake slices and trim the edges so the cake is the same shape as the mold.

Place a small piece of cling film inside the dariole mold, fill it with ice cream and put the mold in the freezer.

In a medium bowl, whisk the egg whites until they form stiff peaks. Slowly add half the sugar and the cream of tartar and whisk again. Slowly add the rest of the sugar and whisk. The meringue should start to look smooth and glossy after 3 to 5 minutes.

Remove the ice cream dariole molds from the freezer and pop the ice cream on top of the cake slices, removing the cling wrap from the ice cream. Quickly spread the meringue thickly over the ice cream and sponge cake.

Bake for 3 to 4 minutes and serve immediately.

LEARNING POINTS

- The ice cream stays frozen because the meringue and sponge cake don't conduct heat very well, which means the heat from the oven doesn't reach the ice cream. The meringue insulates the ice cream from the heat of the oven.
- The meringue and cake are full of air bubbles, which make them great insulators.

DENSITY ICE LOLLIES

There's nothing like a homemade ice lolly (popsicle) on a hot day. The flavor options are almost endless: you can use flavored water, juice, smoothies or even flavored milk with any number of extra ingredients to make the ice lollies special, such as sprinkles, gummy bears or small pieces of fruit.

This activity demonstrates how different liquids can have different densities while creating a super tasty ice lolly.

INGREDIENTS

Thick smoothie

Fruit juice

SUPPLIES

Popsicle mold

Fill the popsicle mold halfway with the thick smoothie and gently pour the juice over the top. The juice should sit on top of the smoothie as it is less dense.

Carefully place the ice lollies in the freezer for 2 hours, or until they are frozen.

Remove the ice lollies from the mold. You should find you have a beautiful layered ice lolly.

MORE FUN

- Add small pieces of fruit or chopped candy to the lollies as you make them and watch where they settle.
- Try adding melted chocolate and sprinkles over the top of the ice lollies. Remember to let the chocolate cool before spreading it over the frozen ice lollies or they might start to melt.

LEARNING POINTS

- *Density* refers to how much mass there is in a certain space. Imagine the inside of a cookie jar. If there are two cookies inside, the cookie jar has a certain density. If you add five more cookies, the density increases as the mass has increased, but the size of the space in the cookie jar has stayed the same.
- If you've tried adding solids to your ice lolly, where did they settle? They probably dropped to the bottom of the mold. This happens because the pieces of fruit or candy are denser than the juice and smoothie, so they drop through those layers.

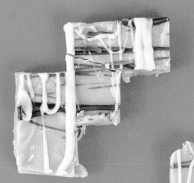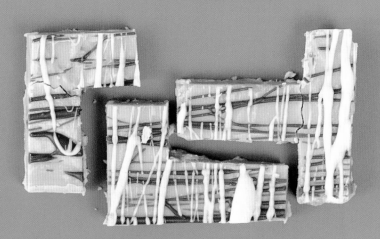

All candy is made from sugar syrup, but the texture of each type is different. Texture depends on the size of the sugar crystals and the sugar concentration.

It is the concentration of sugar that changes the hardness of candy. For example, when toffee is made, the sugar mixture is boiled and heated to around 300°F (150°C), which means most of the water has evaporated, yielding a higher sugar concentration.

In this activity, you're going to heat the sugary mixture to a lower temperature to see the effect of a higher water content and lower sugar concentration on the taste and feel of the candy.

 Adult Supervision

FUDGE TETRIS

INGREDIENTS

¾ cup plus 1½ tbsp (200 ml) condensed milk

13 oz (370 g) white chocolate

Pure vanilla extract (optional)

1¾ oz (50 g) chocolate or candy melts (optional)

SUPPLIES

Medium rimmed baking sheet

Parchment paper

Medium pot

Wooden spoon

Candy thermometer

Small microwave-safe or heatproof bowl

Spoon

Knife

MORE FUN

- To test whether the fudge mixture is at the right temperature, carefully drop a small ball of the mixture into cold water. A soft ball of fudge should form. Don't take this ball out of the water immediately, as it will be very hot.

Line a medium rimmed baking sheet with parchment paper and set it aside.

Place the condensed milk and white chocolate in a medium pot over low heat. Melt until the chocolate completely dissolves.

Increase the heat and bring the mixture to a boil. Reduce the heat and simmer for about 10 minutes, stirring continuously with a wooden spoon.

The temperature of the fudge at this stage should read about 240°F (115°C) on a candy thermometer.

Turn off the heat, add a drop of vanilla to the mixture (if using) and keep stirring until the mixture becomes sticky and starts to set. This will take 2 to 3 minutes.

Pour the fudge into the baking sheet and let it cool completely.

If desired, place the chocolate or candy melts in a small bowl and melt the chocolate in 20-second intervals in the microwave or over a pot of simmering water, stirring frequently.

Once the fudge is cool, remove it from the baking sheet. Use a spoon to drizzle the melted chocolate over the top of the fudge. Leave to fully set.

Once the chocolate is hard, carefully cut the fudge into Tetris shapes with a knife.

Split the Tetris fudge pieces between players and start the game. The winner is the first to add all their fudge to the game area.

LEARNING POINTS

- Sugar syrup goes through several stages when boiled. The temperature at which you stop boiling the mixture depends on the type of candy you want to make. Fudge needs to be cooked to the soft-ball stage as it is soft, but if you wanted a hard candy you'd heat the mixture for a longer amount of time to get to the soft-crack or hard-crack stage.

MARSHMALLOW TREAT JENGA®

Who can win the most marshmallow treats? Who will make the tower tumble? Play against your friends to find out.

Use a bigger pan than you think you might need for the marshmallows, as they expand when heated because they contain a lot of air, which expands when warmed.

INGREDIENTS

3 tbsp plus 1 tsp (50 g) butter, chopped into small pieces

6¾ oz (200 g) marshmallows

4¾ oz (140 g) puffed rice cereal

Powdered sugar

SUPPLIES

Medium pot

Wooden spoon

Large baking pan

Parchment paper

Knife

Sieve

Place the butter and marshmallows in a medium pot and heat over low heat, stirring continuously with a wooden spoon until melted.

Turn off the heat and carefully pour the puffed rice cereal into the pot. Mix well.

Line a large baking pan with parchment paper, leaving enough overhang at the ends to cover the top as well.

Pour the marshmallow mixture into the baking pan and cover it with the overhanging parchment paper. Carefully press down to flatten the marshmallow mixture. Refrigerate for 2 hours to allow the marshmallow treat to set.

Remove the baking pan from the fridge and slice the marshmallow treat into Jenga-size pieces with a knife. You should find the surface is sticky, so lightly dust the tops and bottoms of the pieces with powdered sugar using a sieve.

Build your Jenga tower and start to play.

MORE FUN

- Can you make the marshmallow treats extra special by adding some popping candy?

- If you cover the marshmallow treats in chocolate, are they easier or harder to remove from the Jenga tower?

- Try microwaving a marshmallow for 30 seconds. It will grow to about four times its original size!

LEARNING POINTS

- Marshmallows are mostly sugar, water and air bubbles. When you heat a marshmallow in the microwave, the water in it heats up, which warms the sugar and air bubbles. The sugar softens, so when the air bubbles expand the marshmallow puffs up.

BUILD

Indulge your inner Willy Wonka by building a chocolate bridge reinforced with wafers or licorice, whip up pancake mixes with different ingredients to find the one which gives you the biggest stack, design and make a boat to save cereal from milk and find the best edible foundation for a toothpick house as well as other exciting, creative, food-based engineering projects.

Give yourself time to play, tinker, explore and build with these fun activities. How long can you build a breadstick bridge, what height will your messy meringue tower reach and which syrup will stick a veggie stack together the best?

The creative and imaginative opportunities are endless. Skim through the pages and choose your favorite to try first—maybe you could even combine two activities together. How about a breadstick bridge on a Jell-O® foundation or a mini pancake tower versus meringue tower build-off?

Don't forget, once you've finished that you can eat your creation. Just don't eat the eggshells—they might be a bit crunchy!

 Adult Supervision

TALLEST PANCAKE TOWER

Do you like your pancakes thick and fluffy or thin and chewy? Whether you use baking powder is the key to creating your ideal breakfast.

Most pancake recipes include flour, something to sweeten the batter (such as sugar or honey), milk and oil. Baking powder is used in cooking to make things rise, as it produces carbon dioxide when mixed with water. It is the bubbles of carbon dioxide that make the pancakes rise.

Too much flour makes pancakes thick and dry and not enough makes the batter too runny. Milk gives them moisture and oil helps them cook evenly.

INGREDIENTS

1 cup (125 g) all-purpose flour

2 tbsp (24 g) superfine (caster) sugar

1 tbsp (15 ml) oil

1 cup (240 ml) milk

2 tsp (8 g) baking powder

Oil, for frying

Pancake toppings (optional)

SUPPLIES

2 medium bowls

Wooden spoon

Medium skillet

Ruler

In a medium bowl, mix together the flour, sugar, oil and milk. Stir with a wooden spoon until the batter is smooth.

Transfer half the batter to another medium bowl. Add the baking powder to one bowl of batter.

Heat the oil in a medium skillet over medium heat. Add ½ cup (120 ml) of batter to the skillet. Cook the pancake for 2 minutes on each side, or until the pancake is a light golden-brown color. Repeat this process until all the batter is gone.

Create a pancake stack for each half of the batter—a stack of pancakes with baking powder and a stack of pancakes without baking powder—and measure how tall they are with a ruler. Sprinkle the pancake toppings over your stack, if desired.

MORE FUN

- Pancakes made without an ingredient to make them rise are known as crepes. Crepes are thinner pancakes that can be rolled, making them a great dessert option: Try spreading strawberry compote or another fruity filling over a crepe and rolling it up.

- Baking powder is made from baking soda, cream of tartar and cornstarch. When water is added, it produces a gas (carbon dioxide). You can watch this happen by putting 1 tablespoon (12 g) of baking powder in a small container and adding a little water.

LEARNING POINTS

- Baking powder is a leavening agent, which makes the pancakes rise as they cook. You should have found that the pancakes without baking powder didn't rise as much.

- Baking powder is used in pancakes instead of baking soda as baking soda needs an acid to activate it and there's no acid in the ingredients.

BREADSTICK BRIDGE

If you like soft breadsticks with a crunchy exterior, this is the recipe for you. The addition of yeast makes the dough rise and gives the breadsticks a slightly airy inside while the cinnamon sugar topping adds a sweet crunch to the creation.

Once you've finished baking, use the breadsticks to make a bridge and see what you can balance on top before it breaks.

Think about how to make the structure stable so it doesn't topple easily.

INGREDIENTS

4½ cups (450 g) bread flour

2 tsp (7 g) dried instant yeast

Pinch of salt

1 cup plus 2 tsp (250 ml) warm water

Vegetable oil or melted butter

6 tbsp (54 g) brown sugar

4 tsp (12 g) ground cinnamon

SUPPLIES

Large bowl

Parchment paper

Kitchen towel

Large baking sheet

Pastry brush

Small bowl

Wire rack

Place the flour, yeast and salt in a large bowl, and add the water slowly until you have a soft dough that is not sticky. Knead the dough for 5 to 10 minutes.

Divide the dough into about 20 balls and roll each into a long sausage shape.

Place the breadsticks on a large piece of parchment paper and cover them with a kitchen towel. Leave the breadsticks in a warm place for about 1 hour. The breadsticks should increase in size.

Preheat the oven to 355°F (180°C).

Transfer the parchment paper and breadsticks to a large baking sheet. Lightly brush each breadstick with a little oil using a pastry brush.

Mix together the brown sugar and cinnamon in a small bowl and sprinkle the cinnamon sugar evenly over the breadsticks.

Bake the breadsticks for 12 minutes, or until they are golden brown.

Place the breadsticks on a wire rack until they are cool.

Construct a bridge with the breadsticks. Can you balance fruit or large toy cars on top of it?

MORE FUN

- Try this with store-bought breadsticks. Are they easier to use?

LEARNING POINTS

- Experiment with different bases for your breadstick bridge. A thicker base will be stabler.
- Try adding extra supports so the bridge can hold more weight.

EGGSHELL BRIDGE

If you've ever accidentally dropped an egg, you probably think the shell is weak and brittle, but in the correct circumstances an eggshell can be very strong because of its shape. A half eggshell is a dome, which is a strong shape.

Triangles, arches and domes are all strong shapes and are used by engineers to make structures stable.

SUPPLIES

4 eggs
Small container
Pen
Clear tape
Scissors (optional)
Cardboard
Heavy books

Tap the pointed end of each egg carefully on a hard surface to break it and empty out the raw egg into a small container. You can use these to make scrambled eggs later.

Carefully draw a line with a pen around the center of the egg and place clear tape over the line, so the line is in the center of the tape.

Ask an adult to score the egg around the line with scissors.

Very carefully break off pieces of the shell up to the line, or use scissors to cut the eggshell. (If you don't mind the eggshells not being perfectly straight, you can simply pick off small bits of shell until you get a dome shape rather than using the scoring method.)

Place the four half eggshells in a square or rectangle shape and place a piece of thick cardboard over the top. This is your bridge.

Place a stack of books or other heavy objects on top of the cardboard. You should find the eggshells can hold a lot of weight before collapsing.

MORE FUN

- Did you know a fresh egg will sink in water and a stale egg will float?

LEARNING POINTS

- The half eggshells are a dome shape. Domes are very good at spreading weight evenly in all directions so no part of the dome has to support more weight than another part.
- The downward force of the books' weight is balanced by the strong dome shape of the shells, which spreads the load evenly through the eggshells.

TOPPLING TOOTHPICK TOWERS

The Earth's crust is made up of large pieces of rock called tectonic plates. The place where two tectonic plates meet is called a fault. If two plates rub together at a fault, waves of energy (seismic waves) come to the surface of the Earth, and we experience what we term an earthquake.

Earthquakes can be different magnitudes—sometimes they are just small tremors and other times they cause huge amounts of damage to the land above. An earthquake of magnitude 3 would be very small, 6 would cause substantial damage and 9 would have catastrophic effects.

This activity uses things like Jell-O and clay to demonstrate the reason why buildings need strong foundations.

INGREDIENTS

Jell-O

Brownies or soft homemade granola bars

Clay or modeling compound

Gumdrops

SUPPLIES

3 flat trays of the same size and thickness

Toothpicks

Fill each tray with a different foundation to test: Jell-O, brownies and clay. The foundations should all be the same thickness so your investigation is fair.

Build three identical towers using the toothpicks and gumdrops. These should stand up without support.

Place a tower in the center of each foundation and gently shake each tray using the same amount of force. Record how many shakes it takes for each tower to collapse. If after three shakes the tower is still standing, try shaking the tray harder.

MORE FUN

• Try the investigation again using taller towers. What's the tallest tower you can build without it falling over?

• If you make the foundations thicker, they should be stronger. Design an investigation to test this.

LEARNING POINTS

• If an earthquake happens at the bottom of the sea, it can push water upward, creating huge waves called tsunamis.

• A seismometer is used to measure the magnitude of an earthquake. Earthquakes are measured on the Richter scale.

• Movement of a tectonic plate of just 8 inches (20 cm) is enough to set off an earthquake!

MESSY MERINGUE STRUCTURES

It's hard to believe that fluffy meringue is made from egg whites, but thanks to the addition of air from whisking and the disruption of the tightly curled protein chains in the egg whites, you can make a delicious dessert that barely resembles its ingredients.

Proteins are made up from smaller compounds called amino acids. Some amino acids are attracted to water while others are repelled. Whisking egg white adds air to the mixture. The amino acids repelled by water attach to the air. The more the mixture is mixed or whisked, the more amino acid–covered bubbles are created, making the mixture fluff up.

INGREDIENTS

4 egg whites

1 cup plus 2 tsp (200 g) superfine (caster) sugar

Whipped cream

Strawberries or raspberries

SUPPLIES

2 large baking sheets

Parchment paper

Large glass or metal bowl

Electric hand mixer

MORE FUN

- The sugar acts as a stabilizer, helping the amino acids bond together. Can you try making a meringue without sugar to investigate whether it makes a difference to the taste, look or structure of the meringue?

- Try baking a flat sheet of meringue and investigating how much fruit it can hold before collapsing.

Preheat the oven to 225°F (110°C).

Line 2 large baking sheets with parchment paper.

Put the egg whites in a large bowl and use the electric hand mixer to whisk them slowly at first, then faster as they expand. When the mixture forms stiff peaks, the egg whites are ready. Slowly add the sugar, a few tablespoons (24 to 36 g) at a time, and whisk after each addition.

You should end up with a shiny white mixture that holds its shape.

To make small meringues, place 2 heaping tablespoons (14 g) of the egg white mixture onto the parchment paper of each tray. Remember to leave space between the meringues.

Place the baking sheets in the oven for about 1 hour and then leave the meringues to cool.

Once the meringues are cool, use the whipped cream and strawberries to build meringue towers.

Do some meringue shapes work better than others? Look carefully at the size and shape of each one to build a stable structure, using the whipped cream to stick them together.

LEARNING POINTS

- Did you know that only egg whites are used to make meringue as egg yolks contain fat, which interferes with how the egg white proteins arrange themselves, stopping the mixture from fluffing up?

- Once whipped up, egg whites cannot return to their original consistency. Whisking completely denatures the proteins, which means they lose their shape permanently.

VEGGIE STACKS

Create a colorful, healthy centerpiece for a party with chopped vegetables. Just don't forget to warn the guests that the tower could tumble at any moment!

INGREDIENTS

Carrots

Cucumbers

Cherry tomatoes

Bell peppers

Celery

Asparagus

Hummus

Maple syrup

Greek yogurt

SUPPLIES

Knife

Plate or cutting board

Ask an adult to carefully chop the vegetables into long rectangular shapes if possible. This will be harder with some vegetables than others.

On a plate or cutting board, construct three identical towers—one with hummus, one with maple syrup and one with Greek yogurt between the vegetables. You could lay a foundation of hummus, maple syrup or Greek yogurt and build on top, or have the vegetables as the foundation. Leave the towers to set for about 30 minutes.

Gently shake the plate or cutting board. Does the tower tumble? Remember to either construct all three towers on the same base or shake each tower with the same force to make it a fair test.

Try again, but this time make the base of each tower wider—you should find it's stabler.

MORE FUN

• Try building a vegetable model of a famous tower.

LEARNING POINTS

• Think about the shape of each vegetable. Cubed carrots will make a better base than cherry tomatoes, for example.

SAVE THE CEREAL

Have you ever left your lovely, crunchy cereal in milk for a bit too long and found it to be all soggy as you finish? This is because the cereal absorbs milk from the bowl.

In this activity, you're going to design a boat to save your cereal from a soggy end!

INGREDIENTS

Different types of cereal
Milk
Lime, halved and flesh removed
Bell pepper, halved
Slice of bread

SUPPLIES

Muffin pan
Cereal bowl

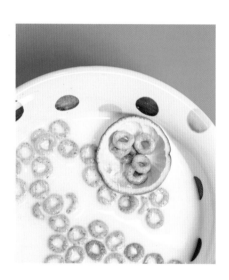

Feel each type of cereal and try to break each one; you should find they're brittle and easy to snap.

Taste the cereals and write down how crunchy they are on a scale of 1 to 10.

Pour a small amount of milk into each well of a muffin pan and add a different type of cereal to each well. Check the cereal every 2 minutes and compare what happens to each cereal type.

Does the crunchiness affect how fast the cereal turns to mush?

Design a boat or raft to save some of your cereal from the milk. You could try a half lime skin (wash it thoroughly), half a bell pepper or a slice of bread. Think about how well each might work.

To test your boat, fill a cereal bowl three-quarters full of milk and place the boat on top. If it floats, add some cereal to the boat.

MORE FUN

- You should find that a sugar-coated cereal absorbs less milk, as the milk has to break down the sugar coating before reaching the cereal. Repeat the investigation using different types of sugar-coated cereals with a non–sugar-coated cereal as the control.

LEARNING POINTS

- You should find that the lime and bell pepper boats protect the cereal better than bread. This is because lime and peppers have a waterproof coating whereas bread will absorb the milk and eventually break down.

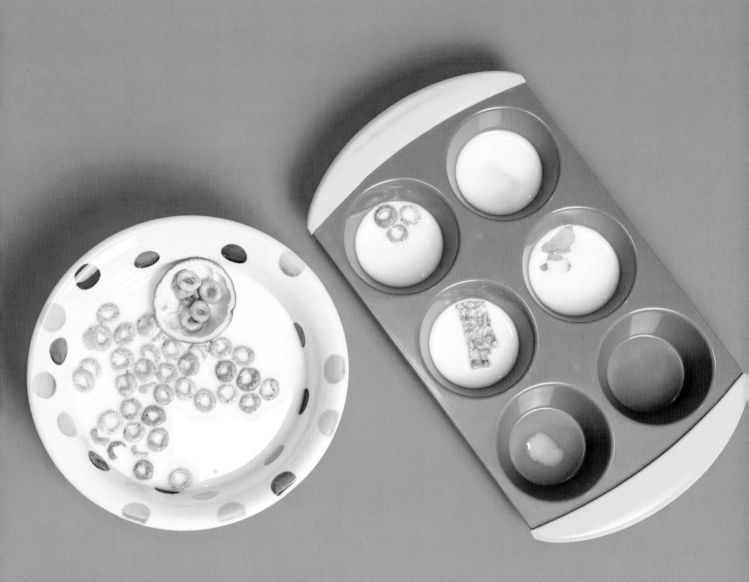

Adult Supervision

CHOCOLATE BRIDGE

If you love chocolate, this is the activity for you. Design, build and test a chocolate bridge to discover how you can strengthen it.

Choose your favorite extra ingredients to make the bridge stronger. Licorice or wafers are good things to try first.

INGREDIENTS
6¾ oz (200 g) chocolate
Licorice or thin snack wafers

SUPPLIES
Medium heatproof bowl
Parchment paper
Wooden spoon
Blocks
Small toys

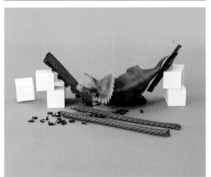

Gently melt the chocolate in a medium heatproof bowl over a pot of simmering water.

Lay the parchment paper out on a table and use a wooden spoon to gently form the chocolate into rectangle shapes on the paper. Each rectangle will form a separate bridge. Try to use the same amount of chocolate for each bridge.

Before the chocolate sets, gently place the licorice or wafers into the chocolate and leave it to harden. Think about which way you want the strengthening candy to lie. Leave one rectangle as plain chocolate. This is your control bridge.

Set up two identical stacks of blocks to be the base of the bridge and place a chocolate bridge on top.

Start with the blocks close together and gently place the toys on top in the middle. If the bridge can hold the weight, move the blocks to the ends of the bridge and try again. Record how many toys the bridge can hold before breaking.

Test each bridge in the same way to discover which is the strongest.

MORE FUN
• Test a bridge with the candy lying along the length of the bridge and also cut into segments lying across the width of a bridge. Which orientation do you think will make the bridge the strongest?

LEARNING POINTS
• When setting up a scientific investigation, you always need a control. In this activity, the control bridge is the plain chocolate bridge and the variables being tested are the extra ingredients in the chocolate of the other test bridges.
• You should find the bridges with extra reinforcements are stronger than just plain chocolate.

SUPER STRONG GINGERBREAD HOUSES

These gingerbread houses are very easy to make and can be decorated for any time of year. Add white icing sugar that looks like snow in winter or green icing for leaves in spring or summer, or try a spooky Halloween theme for autumn.

Test different strengths of icing to discover which holds the house together best.

INGREDIENTS

½ cup plus 1 tsp (75 g) brown sugar

2 tbsp (30 ml) golden syrup

1 tsp ground ginger

1 tsp ground cinnamon

1 tbsp (15 ml) water, plus more as needed

6 tbsp plus 1 tsp (95 g) butter

1¾ cups plus 2 tsp (225 g) all-purpose flour

½ tsp baking soda

Powdered sugar

Decorations

SUPPLIES

Medium pot

Wooden spoon

Sieve

2 medium bowls

Cling film

Large baking sheet

Parchment paper

Rolling pin

Knife

Wire rack

Put the brown sugar, golden syrup, ginger, cinnamon and water in a medium pot and bring the mixture to a boil over medium heat.

Remove the pot from the heat, add the butter and stir with a wooden spoon until it is completely melted. Leave the mixture to cool for 5 minutes.

Sift the flour and baking soda into a bowl with a sieve.

Slowly stir the flour into the syrup mixture and knead until you have a smooth dough.

Place the mixture in a medium bowl, cover the dough with cling film and leave the bowl somewhere cool for about 30 minutes.

Meanwhile, preheat the oven to 355°F (180°C). Line a large baking sheet with parchment paper.

Roll out the dough, cut it into 6 equal rectangle or square shapes and place the pieces on the baking sheet. Bake the gingerbread for 10 to 15 minutes.

Remove the gingerbread from the oven and place the pieces on a wire rack to cool. If the gingerbread has lost its square shape, cut the sides so they are straight again.

While the gingerbread cools, make three different thicknesses of icing by adding different amounts of water to the powdered sugar. Make one runny, one thick and one somewhere in the middle.

(continued)

SUPER STRONG GINGERBREAD HOUSES (CONT.)

Construct the house very simply by making an A shape with 2 gingerbread pieces, with the icing holding the pieces together. Create 1 house for each type of icing.

Once the icing has set, test how stable each house is by holding it upside down and gently shaking it.

Decorate the strongest house with the rest of the icing and small decorations.

MORE FUN

- Can you make a bigger version of your gingerbread house?
- Try a viscosity race with the icings—you should find the thickest icing (the most viscous) travels the most slowly.

LEARNING POINTS

- Powdered sugar is very finely ground sugar with about 3 percent cornstarch added. The cornstarch stops the sugar from clumping together when water is added and makes it flow more smoothly. If you add a little water to cornstarch and let it run through your fingers, you can feel how smoothly it flows. Cornstarch and water is known as oobleck and makes a great goo or slime!

Decorate your house.

Use thick icing to construct the house.

Use leftover ingredients to make decorations for the house.

EXPLORE

Have you ever wondered what makes up the cells in your body, what DNA looks like and what lies under the top layer of soil? This chapter uses cakes and candy to model things you probably didn't even know existed. Just don't eat your creations too quickly!

Find out about the science of sugar while making a fudge model of the Earth and learn about the rest of the planets in our solar system with toffee apple planets. You'll have a completely edible solar system before you know it.

Test your knowledge of 3-D shapes with some fruity kebabs and try your hand at color mixing while making colorful candy rocks. If you don't have a sweet tooth, the Seasons Pizza (page 88) is sure to be a hit and would make a great meal for the whole family.

Adult Supervision

LAYERS-OF-THE-EARTH FUDGE

If you could slice through the Earth, you'd see several different layers. The top layer is called the crust. This is the thinnest layer and is made up of different types of rocks.

Next is the upper mantle, which makes up most of our planet. The mantle moves very slowly and it is this movement that is a main cause of earthquakes.

The outer core is a thick, fluid layer, mostly made up of molten iron.

The hot, metal ball that makes up the inner core is made up mostly of iron and is only solid because of the incredible amount of pressure it's under.

This fudgy Earth layer model demonstrates the different layers of our Earth using colored fudge.

INGREDIENTS

2¼ cups + 2 tbsp (200 ml) condensed milk

13 oz (370 g) white chocolate, chopped

Red, orange, yellow, blue and green food coloring

SUPPLIES

Medium pot

Wooden spoon

Candy thermometer (optional)

Medium bowl

Knife

Place the condensed milk and white chocolate in a medium pot and heat gently over low heat, stirring continuously with a wooden spoon until the chocolate is almost melted. If you have a candy thermometer, it should read about 240°F (115°C) at this point.

Turn off the heat and stir the mixture until the chocolate is completely melted and the consistency is smooth. Pour the fudge into a medium bowl and let it cool for about 30 minutes. Try making a small ball out of some fudge. The fudge needs to be moldable, as you need it to stay in a ball shape and not flatten out. If the mixture is too soft to stay in a ball shape, wait another 30 minutes and try again.

To make the Earth's inner core, take a marble-size amount of fudge and add a little red food coloring. Mix with your hands until the fudge is completely colored and roll it into a ball. Place the ball in the fridge until it is solid.

To make the Earth's outer core, add a little orange food coloring to enough fudge to wrap around the inner core. Once it is colored, mold it around the inner core and place it in the fridge again until set.

Repeat the preceding steps for the Earth's mantle, using yellow food coloring.

To make the Earth's crust, make some blue fudge and green fudge and gently mix them to give an Earth-like appearance. Wrap the crust around the mantle and leave the fudge to harden in the fridge.

Once the fudge is set, ask an adult to slice the fudgy Earth with a knife to reveal the layers!

LEARNING POINTS

• When you are cooking with sugar, 240°F (115°C) is the soft-ball stage. At this stage, there is still some water left in the mixture and if you dropped a little of the sugar syrup into cold water it would form a soft, moldable ball.

MORE FUN

• Try making a cell model with fudge (see the Cell Model Cupcakes on page 92).

CANDY DNA MODEL

DNA stands for *deoxyribonucleic acid*, a long, thin molecule a bit like a recipe containing instructions or code that tells cells how to behave and grow.

James Watson and Francis Crick, along with Maurice Wilkins and Rosalind Franklin, discovered the structure of DNA in 1953. Before this exciting discovery, scientists knew that DNA carried genes that parents passed onto their offspring but they didn't know how it worked or what DNA looked like.

DNA is made from nucleotides with two backbones holding them together. The backbones twist around to form a double-helix shape. The two strands are held together by hydrogen bonds between the base (nucleotide) pairs.

There are four different nucleotides: adenine, thymine, cytosine and guanine. We call these bases and usually refer to them by the first letter of their names: A pairs with T and G with C.

INGREDIENTS

Gumdrops in 4 different colors

Licorice sticks or other long, thin candy

SUPPLIES

Toothpicks

Remember, C and G and T and A always pair up, so assign a color to each nucleotide and add pairs of sweets to your toothpicks.

Attach each end of the toothpicks to licorice sticks, spacing them out evenly.

Once you have a long enough string, twist it to give the spiral shape of a double helix.

MORE FUN

- DNA can copy itself by separating a bit like a zipper on a coat. The newly unpaired nucleotides attract new partners, building two new identical helices. Can you model this in the same way?

LEARNING POINTS

- Did you know that 99.9 percent of the DNA of each person is the same? It's just that tiny 0.1 percent that makes us all different! Isn't that incredible?

Everything around us has three dimensions: height, length and width. But when we draw objects, we usually show them in two dimensions. A flat shape has two dimensions, length and width.

Flat shapes are called 2-D shapes. If you see a picture of a ball in a book, it's a circle shape—but an actual ball is a 3-D shape called a sphere, because it has three dimensions.

Adult Supervision

FRUITY 3-D SHAPES

If you look around your kitchen, you'll find lots of examples of 3-D shapes. A can of food is a cylinder, oranges and onions are spheres and you probably have cardboard packages that are cubes and cuboids.

This activity uses fruit to make fun 3-D fruity kebabs. Test your friends to discover how many shapes they can recognize.

INGREDIENTS
Fresh fruit (several different types)
Marshmallows (optional)

SUPPLIES
Knife
Melon baller
Wooden skewers

Ask an adult to cut out different 3-D shapes from the fruit with a knife or melon baller (depending on the desired shape). Cubes, cuboids, pyramids, cylinders and spheres are good ones to start with.

Try carefully placing one of each shape on a wooden skewer so you have a 3-D fruity kebab.

Add marshmallows between some of the 3-D fruit shapes for an extra special treat.

Try putting the shapes together. Can you create a bigger cube from the small cubes? Or a cuboid from several squares?

MORE FUN
- Can you work out how many faces, edges and vertices each of your fruity shapes has?
- Which fruity kebab has the most vertices?
- Look around the house and try to find something the same shape as your fruit shapes.

LEARNING POINTS
- 3-D shapes have faces, edges and vertices. Faces are the sides of the shape and are flat or curved surfaces. Vertices are corners where edges meet.
- Edges are where 2 faces meet. A cube has 12 edges, 6 faces and 8 vertices! A cuboid has the same number of edges, vertices and faces, but 4 of its sides are rectangles, not squares.

Adult Supervision

COLOR-MIXING CANDY ROCKS

Did you know you can make all the colors of the rainbow from just three colors? Red, yellow and blue are known as primary colors, as they cannot be made by mixing two other colors.

There are lots of ways to test this out. Try mixing paint to see how many colors you can make or add a little food coloring to water and mix colors that way.

This activity uses hard colored candies to investigate color mixing. As the candy melts, the different colors mix together.

INGREDIENTS

A variety of hard candies, such as Jolly Ranchers and clear mints

Edible glitter (optional)

SUPPLIES

Small plastic or paper bags

Rolling pin or mallet

Medium baking sheet

Parchment paper

Preheat the oven to 480°F (250°C).

Sort each color candy into a separate plastic bag and fold the bag over to seal it.

Carefully crush the candy with a rolling pin or mallet. Don't crush it into dust—it's best to have lots of different sizes.

Line a medium baking sheet with parchment paper and add about 1 teaspoon of each color candy you want to mix in circle shapes, making sure some of the different colors overlap.

Place the candy in the oven for about 5 minutes, or until completely melted.

This is a good time to sprinkle the candy with edible glitter if you want sparkly rocks.

Let the candy rocks cool before touching them.

MORE FUN

- Can you make candy rocks where the colors stay separate? Try placing a clear candy between the colors.

- Can you make the candy into a lollipop?

LEARNING POINTS

- There are three primary colors that cannot be created by mixing other colors: red, yellow and blue.

- Secondary colors can be made by mixing primary colors:

  Yellow + blue = green

  Red + yellow = orange

  Blue + red = purple

- Tertiary colors are made by mixing a primary color with a secondary color.

Have you ever spotted an animal footprint and wondered what type of animal left it?

Studying and identifying animal prints is something humans have been doing for a very long time. Footprints hold clues to the type of animal they belong to. Dogs, foxes and wolves have four toes on the front and back feet with claws you can see in the print. Cats also have four toes but retract their claws, making their footprints different.

This activity uses toy animals to make footprints in cookies, but you could also make your own footprints in snow or by wetting the bottom of your shoes. Trying running to see how the footprint pattern changes.

 Adult Supervision

COOKIE FOOTPRINTS

INGREDIENTS

Cookie dough (such as the Basic Cookie recipe on page 137)

Melted chocolate, sprinkles or other decorations (optional)

SUPPLIES

Medium baking sheet

Parchment paper

Plastic dinosaurs or other toy animals

Preheat the oven to 355°F (180°C). Line a medium baking sheet with parchment paper.

Divide the cookie dough into about 12 evenly sized balls and squash them down so they are flat.

Clean the plastic dinosaurs' feet and press them firmly into the dough so you have a footprint shape.

Bake the cookies in the oven for 15 to 20 minutes, or until golden brown. If the footprints fade too much after baking, press the dinosaurs' feet in the cookies again while they are hot.

You can either leave the cookies as they are or fill the footprints with melted chocolate or sprinkles.

MORE FUN

• Bake some cupcakes and cover them with thick icing, then press the dinosaurs' feet into the icing to give you footprint cupcakes.

LEARNING POINTS

• If you find a real animal print, measure the length and width of several prints—you might find the front feet are bigger as they support more of the animal's weight.

• Count the number of toes and look for claw marks.

• If you can see lots of prints, you could even measure the length between prints to give you the stride of the animal.

• Did you know some dinosaurs had different numbers of toes on their front and back feet?

When you think of soil, you probably think of the layer of mud where you plant flowers and where worms and other animals live. Did you know there are several layers of soil, and soil is not just mud or dirt but a mixture of decayed plants and animals, minerals and small pieces of rock?

This activity uses different types of cake to model the layers that make up soil. You can bake the cakes yourself or use store-bought varieties.

Soil is made up of the following layers:

- Organic layer (a thick layer of plant remains, such as leaves and twigs)
- Topsoil (a thin layer 5- to 10-inches [13- to 25-cm] thick, organic matter and minerals where plants and organisms live)
- Subsoil (clay, iron and organic matter)
- Parent material (upper layers develop from this later; it's mostly made up of large rocks)
- Bedrock (several feet below the surface, a solid mass of rock)

CAKE SOIL LAYERS

INGREDIENTS

Different types of cake

Green icing

Ready-to-roll brown fondant icing (optional)

Gummy worms

SUPPLIES

Icing bag

Rolling pin

MORE FUN

- Can you make an Earth layer cake? Try using different colored sponge cake to represent each layer.

To make a cake model of soil layers, you need to think about the look and texture of each layer and build from the bottom layer upward.

How about a nutty granola bar for the bedrock layer, followed by a nutty cake for the parent layer?

The subsoil layer needs to have fewer rocks and needs to be a lighter color than the topsoil.

Once you've built up the layers of cake, use an icing bag to pipe green icing onto the top to represent grass and leaves.

With a rolling pin, roll the brown fondant icing into a long, thin shape and use this to model sticks and roots in the cake. Place gummy worms among the sticks and roots.

LEARNING POINTS

- Soil plays a huge role in supporting life on our planet. Plants not only grow and support themselves in soil but also absorb nutrients to grow using their roots.
- Many small organisms live in soil, such as earthworms, ants, beetles and flies.
- Soil also affects our atmosphere by releasing carbon dioxide.
- Did you know that in just 1 teaspoon of soil there can be several hundred million bacteria?

Can you create a pizza to show each season of the year?

The year is made up of four different seasons: spring, summer, autumn and winter. The weather is different during each season. As the seasons and weather change, plants change and animals change how they behave.

In spring, the weather starts to get warmer after a cold winter—trees start to grow new leaves and flowers start to appear again. Summer usually has long, hot days before a milder autumn when leaves change color to red, orange and yellow before falling off completely for winter when the days are short and trees bare. Use this knowledge to create a four-season pizza!

Adult Supervision

SEASONS PIZZA

INGREDIENTS

Pizza sauce

Pizza crust (page 34)

Shredded cheddar cheese

Bell peppers

Olives, sliced

Mozzarella cheese

Chicken or pepperoni

Arugula or other greens

Broccoli florets

Chilis, finely chopped

Bacon

Cherry tomatoes, sliced

Mushrooms, sliced

SUPPLIES

Pizza stone or baking sheet

Preheat the oven to 355°F (180°C).

Spread the pizza sauce over the pizza crust and sprinkle a thin layer of cheddar cheese over the whole pizza.

Imagine the pizza is split into quarters and use your toppings to decorate each quarter to look like a season using the bell peppers, olives, mozzarella cheese, chicken or pepperoni, arugula, broccoli, chilis, bacon, cherry tomatoes and mushrooms. For example, how about yellow bell peppers to represent the sun, green bell peppers for leaves and plants, olives for the bleaker winter months and mozzarella snowman and snow? Or try chicken or pepperoni for the trunk of a tree covered with green arugula leaves in summer, red and yellow bell peppers in autumn and bare in winter.

Bake the pizza for 10 to 12 minutes and enjoy your season slices.

MORE FUN

- Can you add some animals to your pizza? How about a hedgehog hibernating in winter, a squirrel collecting nuts in autumn or bees buzzing around in summer?

LEARNING POINTS

- The Earth spins on an axis as it orbits the sun tiled at an angle. It's this tilt that gives us seasons. As the Earth travels around the sun, either the Northern or Southern Hemispheres are nearer the sun. The hemisphere nearest the sun is in summer while the other half is in winter.

- The northern and southern parts of Earth have different seasons at the same time. For example, Europe's winter is Australia's summer. This is because the southern part of the Earth is nearest the sun at that point.

- Places near the middle of the Earth are hot all year, as they get the same strength of sunlight year-round.

 **Adult Supervision**

TOFFEE APPLE PLANETS

Create a toffee apple solar system that's interesting to look at and fun to eat!

There are eight planets in the solar system: Mercury, Venus, Earth and Mars are the inner planets, and Jupiter, Saturn, Uranus and Neptune are the larger outer planets.

Toffee apple planets are a fun way to model the solar system. As apples don't vary much in size, we're not going to model the solar system accurately to scale, but think about how the planets look in space.

INGREDIENTS

8 apples (a mixture of small and large)

1 cup plus 2 tsp (400 g) superfine (caster) sugar

⅓ cup plus 4 tsp (100 ml) water

4 tbsp (60 ml) golden syrup

Food coloring (optional)

Edible glitter (optional)

Sprinkles and other decorations

SUPPLIES

Cake pop or lollipop sticks

Parchment paper

Medium pot

Wooden spoon

Candy thermometer (optional)

Carefully push a cake pop stick into the stem end of each apple. Hold the apples by the stick in the air to ensure they're secure.

Place a large sheet of parchment paper near the stove.

Place the sugar and water in a medium pot over high heat and simmer, stirring frequently with a wooden spoon, until all the sugar dissolves.

Add the golden syrup and cook until the mixture starts to bubble. If you have a candy thermometer, monitor the mixture's temperature—it needs to reach the hard-crack stage, which is 300°F (150°C). If you don't have a candy thermometer, you can test the toffee by using a spoon to drop a small amount of it into cold water. If the toffee hardens instantly in the cold water, it's ready. If it still feels soft, heat it for a few more minutes.

You can add food coloring and edible glitter at this stage, if desired.

Carefully and quickly dip each apple into the toffee mixture, making sure you cover the whole apple. Place the apples, stick side up, on the parchment paper and add sprinkles while the toffee is soft.

Think about what each planet in the solar system looks like and add your decorations accordingly.

MORE FUN

- Make some toffee apple moons. Mars has two moons named Phobos and Deimos—these are both more potato-shaped than spherical.
- Can you make a softer toffee and mold it around the apples?

LEARNING POINTS

- Candy that needs cooking to the hard-crack stage is brittle. This means it feels hard and can snap.
- How hard a candy is depends on how much it was boiled as it was made. There are several stages of candy making: soft-ball, firm-ball, soft-crack and hard-crack.

Adult Supervision

CELL MODEL CUPCAKES

All living things are made up of cells, which are so small they can only be seen with a microscope. Inside cells are structures called organelles, which have special functions.

The cell membrane holds the cell together and controls what can enter and leave the cell. It's a bit like the cell's skin.

The nucleus is like the brain of the cell. It contains DNA, which it uses to instruct the cell how to grow and reproduce.

The cytoplasm is a jelly-like substance that fills the cell and is where chemical reactions occur.

The mitochondria is like the battery of the cell and provides energy.

The lysosomes get rid of waste and also destroy a cell when it dies.

You can make a very simple cell model on a cupcake using a few different sweets.

INGREDIENTS

1 cup (125 g) self-rising flour

8 tbsp plus 1 tsp (125 g) unsalted butter, melted

⅔ cup (125 g) superfine (caster) sugar

2 eggs

1 tsp pure vanilla extract

Red icing

Blue icing

Candy pieces

SUPPLIES

Muffin pan

Paper muffin liners

Large bowl

Electric handheld mixer

Plain white stickers

Toothpicks

Preheat the oven to 355°F (180°C). Line a muffin pan with paper muffin liners.

Add the flour, butter, sugar, eggs and vanilla to a large bowl and mix with a handheld mixer until the batter is smooth.

Divide the mixture between about 10 paper muffin liners and bake for 15 to 20 minutes.

Leave the cupcakes to cool.

Top the cupcakes with either red or blue icing and add candy pieces to represent the organelles.

Label each part of the cell using a white sticker wrapped around a toothpick.

MORE FUN

• Plant cells also have an outer cell wall, which gives the cell extra support; a vacuole, which is a sap-filled space in the cytoplasm; and chloroplasts, which are where photosynthesis occurs. Try to create a model of a plant cell and a nerve cell too.

LEARNING POINTS

• There are many different types of cells. Nerve cells can be very long with connections at each end. These help transport messages around the body. Red blood cells carry oxygen around the body and have no nucleus. Muscle cells are long, thin and bundled up.

Do you know why pretzels are a dark brown and why toast always seem to hit the ground butter-side down? The secret is in a special liquid that pretzel dough is dipped in and the rotation of the toast.

Find out why chia seeds are super, how to stop ketchup from getting stuck in the bottle and why Jell-O doesn't set if you add certain fruits.

Did you know lemons and oranges can sink *and* float? You can even create a drink with some lemon pieces floating and some sinking with your new knowledge.

Discover some science secrets from the kitchen and never get baking soda and baking powder mixed up again with these tasty investigations.

WHY ARE PRETZELS DARK BROWN?

Pretzels are a chewy, soft-centered bread that often have a salty coating, although you can add whatever flavors you want. The dough is very similar to normal bread, but as part of the baking process the pretzel is dipped into an alkaline solution before baking. It is this dunking that stops the pretzel from rising on the outside like regular bread and gives it its chewy, brown crust and typical pretzel flavor.

INGREDIENTS

1½ cups minus 2 tsp (350 ml) lukewarm water

2¼ tsp (7 g) instant yeast

1 tsp salt

1 tbsp (9 g) brown sugar

5 cups (500 g) bread flour

3 tbsp (36 g) baking soda

1¼ cups (300 ml) water

SUPPLIES

2 large bowls

Wooden spoon

Medium baking sheet

Parchment paper

Medium pot

Slotted spoon

MORE FUN

• Try making different flavored pretzel sticks. How about sprinkling them with cinnamon sugar or salt and pepper?

In a large bowl, pour the lukewarm water over the yeast and leave for 2 minutes. Slowly mix in the salt and brown sugar. Add the flour 1 cup (100 g) at a time and mix with a wooden spoon. The dough should no longer be sticky once all the flour is added.

Knead the dough on a floured surface for about 5 minutes, then place it in another large bowl. Cover the bowl and leave it in a warm place for about 15 minutes.

Preheat the oven to 425°F (220°C) and line a medium baking sheet with parchment paper. Roll the dough into a rope and twist it to make a pretzel shape.

Place the baking soda and the water in a medium pot and bring the water to a boil over high heat. Carefully submerge the pretzel in the water and cook for about 30 seconds. Remove it using a slotted spoon.

Let the excess water drain from the pretzel and then place it on the baking sheet.

Bake for about 15 minutes, or until the pretzel is golden brown.

LEARNING POINTS

• When the pretzels are dipped in the baking soda solution, the baking soda starts to react with the surface of the dough, making it turn a yellow color. When the pretzel is baked, the yellow color deepens and becomes the signature shiny brown pretzel color.

• Flour is made up of starch and proteins. One protein called gluten is responsible for the stretchy nature of the dough.

INFLATE A BALLOON WITH BAKING POWDER

Baking soda and baking powder are easily confused in the kitchen as they have a similar function, but they are quite different.

Both baking soda and baking powder are leaveners (that is, they make things rise). They react with other ingredients to produce carbon dioxide gas, which adds bubbles of air to doughs and cake mixtures.

The key difference is that baking soda needs an acid to work, so recipes using baking soda usually have lemon juice, buttermilk or another acidic substance to activate it.

Baking powder doesn't need an acid, as it already has an acid present (usually cream of tartar)—it just needs heat to start working.

INGREDIENTS

1 tbsp (12 g) baking soda
2 tbsp (18 g) cream of tartar
Warm water

SUPPLIES

Small bowl
Small bottle
1 balloon

In a small bowl, mix together the baking soda and cream of tartar. Your baking powder is now ready to use.

Add 2 teaspoons (8 g) of baking powder to a small bottle and pour in a little warm water to activate it. Quickly place a balloon on top and watch it inflate.

MORE FUN

- If you did this with baking soda, nothing would happen as there's no acid to activate the reaction—but try it with vinegar instead of water and you will see some fizz!
- Test your homemade baking powder by making pizza dough (page 34) or breadsticks (page 57).

LEARNING POINTS

- Baking soda contains just one ingredient, sodium bicarbonate. Baking powder contains sodium bicarbonate and cream of tartar (an acid).
- Generally, batters and doughs that use baking soda should be used straightaway as the baking soda starts to work immediately, whereas doughs using baking powder can be stored for a while as they need heat for the baking powder to activate.

SAVE THE GUMMY BEAR

Design a raft or boat to stop a gummy bear from sinking!

Did you know cranberries float? They float because they have air pockets inside. This makes them less dense than water, so they float. The fact that cranberries float make them perfect for creating a raft for a small candy bear.

INGREDIENTS

Gummy bears
Fresh cranberries

SUPPLIES

Large bowl or glass
Water
Toothpicks

Fill the large bowl or glass almost to the top with water. Drop a gummy bear into the container to make sure it sinks.

Design and then build a raft for the gummy bear using only the cranberries and toothpicks. Can you try several different designs?

Test each raft with a gummy bear on top to find the best design.

MORE FUN

- Try other fruits to discover if they float as well as cranberries.
- How many gummy bears can each raft hold?

LEARNING POINTS

Farmers use the fact that cranberries float to help them harvest the berries quickly. They flood the cranberry field to bring the berries to the surface.

Cranberries have air pockets inside.

Build a raft using cranberries and toothpicks.

Test your raft with a gummy bear.

Can you make a cocktail with lemons that float and lemons that have sunk to the bottom of the drink?

Things float when they are less dense than the fluid they are in. Imagine dropping a marble and a table tennis ball into a cup of water. The marble would sink and the table tennis ball would float. This is because the marble is solid with no air pockets (that is, it is dense) and the table tennis ball is full of air (that is, it is not very dense). This is why huge ships can float: They are very heavy, but inside there's a lot of empty space, so they are not very dense.

You probably know that lemons and oranges float on water, but do you know why they float and how you can make them sink? It's all to do with the skin!

Adult Supervision

FRUITY COCKTAILS

INGREDIENTS
Lemon
Orange

SUPPLIES
Large bowl or glass
Water
Knife
Juice, optional

Fill a large bowl or glass halfway with water and drop a lemon into the water. It should float.

Do the same with an orange. This should also float.

Now slice the lemon with a knife and place the slices in a glass of juice or the bowl of water. The slices should still float.

This time, remove the rind from both the lemon and orange. You should find both fruits now sink.

MORE FUN
• Cut the lemon or orange into quarters and slices. Do they sink or float?
• Investigate what happens with a lime. You should find the lime sinks. This is because limes have a thinner rind than lemons with fewer air pockets in the skin. This makes limes denser than lemons.

LEARNING POINTS
• Lemons and oranges float because their skins are filled with tiny pockets of air; this makes them less dense than the water.
• Something else to consider is buoyancy. Generally, the more an object's surface is in contact with water, the more buoyant it is.

SUPER ABSORBING SEEDS

Chia seeds are tiny but can absorb an amazing nine times their weight in liquid! They are often used as an egg replacement in recipes as they become very gelatinous, like the consistency of a raw egg.

Chia seeds are not only helpful in recipes but they are also bursting with nutritional benefits. They are rich in fiber, omega-3 fatty acids, protein and minerals. They really are super seeds.

INGREDIENTS

4 tbsp (40 g) chia seeds
1 cup (240 ml) almond milk
1 tsp honey or pure maple syrup
½ tsp pure vanilla extract
Blueberries, for topping

SUPPLIES

Medium bowl
Spoon
Small bowls

In a medium bowl, combine the chia seeds, almond milk, honey and vanilla. Use a spoon to stir the mixture well. You should find the mixture looks very liquid.

Place the bowl in the fridge for 2 hours, or until the chia mixture is set. You should find it turns into a lovely thick mixture.

Spoon the mixture into smaller bowls and sprinkle the blueberries on top to serve.

MORE FUN

- Try the recipe again, but this time use double the amount of liquid. How is the consistency of the mixture different?
- Create a multicolored dessert by adding melted dark chocolate and different fruit purees to the chia mixture. Layer the different flavors on top of one another.

LEARNING POINTS

- Chia seeds contain a lot of mucilage, which is a type of soluble fiber. One of the functions of mucilage is that the water it absorbs surrounds the seed with moisture, helping germination.

BUTTER-SIDE DOWN?

Have you ever dropped a piece of toast, only for it to land butter-side down and leave a greasy mess on the floor?

Is it just bad luck or is there a reason the toast lands butter-side down? You can find out in this easy investigation.

INGREDIENTS

Bread slices (different thicknesses)
Butter

SUPPLIES

Toaster
Butter knife

With a toaster, toast each slice of bread one by one and butter one side using a butter knife. Drop each slice onto the floor from kitchen-counter height (put a clean mat down, then you can still eat the toast afterward). Record which way each piece of toast lands. Try not to apply any force to the toast—just let it drop out of your hands.

Repeat the investigation, but this time drop the toast from as high as you can reach. Are the results the same?

Try again, but this time drop the toast from counter height and add a little spin.

MORE FUN

• Does untoasted bread also land butter-side down? What about seedy bread?

LEARNING POINTS

• If the toast landed butter-side down by chance, you would expect it to land butter-side down about 50 percent of the time. You should find that when dropped from normal kitchen-counter height, the toast did indeed land butter-side down most of the time. This is because the toast drops at an angle and starts to rotate, but there's only time for it to rotate half a turn, meaning it lands upside down from its starting position.

• If you increase the height from which the toast is dropped, the results should be more varied as the rotation and speed at which the toast falls will change.

BUBBLY ICE CREAM FLOATS

An ice cream float is made by adding a scoop of ice cream to a fizzy drink. Not only does an ice cream float taste delicious but also you'll notice the ice cream makes the soda extra fizzy and frothy. In this activity, you're going to make your very own ice cream float and see the bubbles in action.

INGREDIENTS

Soda

Ice cream

SUPPLIES

Tall glass

Ice cream scoop

Fill a tall glass almost to the top with your favorite soda and carefully place a scoop of ice cream on the top using an ice cream scoop.

Watch what happens. You should see lots of bubbles and froth forming around the ice cream.

MORE FUN

- Try different types of sodas. Do any create more bubbles and froth than others?
- Does it make a difference if the drink is a low-sugar variety?

LEARNING POINTS

- The fizzy drink you use to make the ice cream float contains bubbles of carbon dioxide. When the drink comes into contact with the ice cream, bubbles are released from the fizzy drink, which also helps free air bubbles trapped in the ice cream. As bubbles in ice cream are covered in fat, they expand to give the foamy appearance you see on the surface of the ice cream float.

Carefully add a scoop of ice cream to your soda.

Watch bubbles and froth form around the ice cream.

Do you get different amounts of bubbles and froth with different sodas?

WHY DOESN'T JELL-O® SET?

Have you ever made Jell-O that just won't set? Maybe you added too much water or perhaps it was the addition of another ingredient that interfered with the setting process.

Jell-O contains gelatin, which contains protein molecules. The long protein strands tangle up as they cool down, trapping water to make a solid. Imagine a bowl of spaghetti all jumbled up with water trapped between the strands.

Did you know certain fruits prevent Jell-O from setting? One of these is pineapple.

INGREDIENTS

Jell-O, any flavor

Fresh pineapple, coarsely chopped

Strawberries, bananas or other fruit, coarsely chopped

Canned pineapple, coarsely chopped

SUPPLIES

4 small bowls

Make the Jell-O according to the package instructions.

Divide the liquid Jell-O evenly between 4 small bowls and add fresh pineapple to the first bowl, strawberries to the second bowl and canned pineapple to the third bowl. Do not add any extra ingredients to the Jell-O in the fourth bowl. This is the control. If the Jell-O in this bowl doesn't set, you will know it's something other than the fruit preventing it from setting.

Place the bowls in the fridge for 2 hours to set.

Did the Jell-O set?

MORE FUN

- You should find that the Jell-O with canned pineapple sets. This is because canned pineapple is heated to kill bacteria before placing it in the can. The heating also destroys the enzymes, which would break down the proteins in the gelatin.
- Investigate this concept with other fresh fruits.

LEARNING POINTS

- Pineapple contains an enzyme called bromelain that chops the protein molecules in the Jell-O into smaller pieces, meaning they can't tangle up, so the Jell-O doesn't set. Kiwi contains a similar enzyme called actinidin, which has the same effect.
- Enzymes in your intestines work in the same way, chopping up protein molecules and allowing you to digest food.

IMAGINE

Imagine a cake with raisins that don't sink to the bottom, cress growing with no soil, a fruit salad that doesn't turn brown and ice cubes made from hot water!

Surprise your friends with exploding chocolate popcorn, surprise lollipops and the fizziest lemonade made with a simple kitchen ingredient.

This chapter is all about surprises: Imagine a breakfast of eggs that look like clouds with a sunny yolk on the side. Could there be a better way to start the day?

THE BEST FIZZY LEMONADE

It's a hot day and you really want a glass of lemonade but don't have one in the fridge. What can you do? Make your own! Using the fizzy power of baking soda and with a little bit of clever science, you can even make it ice-cold in minutes.

INGREDIENTS

4 lemons, cut in half, or ½ cup (120 ml) fresh lemon juice

2 cups plus 4 tsp (500 ml) water

2 tsp (8 g) sugar (optional)

1 tsp baking soda

SUPPLIES

Pitcher

Spoon

Squeeze the lemons into the pitcher, getting as much juice out of them as you can.

Add the water and sugar (if using) to the pitcher and mix well with a spoon.

Pour in the baking soda and mix again. You should see bubbles appearing in your lemonade.

MORE FUN

- To cool the lemonade quickly, place the jug in a bowl of ice and salt. Salt lowers the freezing point of ice, making it start to melt. The ice will take heat from the lemonade to melt and cool the lemonade quickly.

- Try using more baking soda to see if the lemonade becomes even fizzier.

LEARNING POINTS

- Baking soda is alkaline, so when it's mixed with the acidic lemon juice, a neutralization reaction occurs. This releases carbon dioxide bubbles, making the lemonade fizzy!

Adult Supervision

ICE CUBES IN A FLASH

Isn't it frustrating when you want a chilled drink but don't have any ice on hand? But did you know you can make ice cubes quickly using hot water? It's not instantaneous, but it's worth a go just to see if it works for you!

Boiled water also gives you a transparent ice cube instead of the cloudy ice you get with tap water.

INGREDIENTS
Water

SUPPLIES
Kettle
Ice cube tray

Bring a kettle of water to a boil, then remove it from the heat and leave it to cool for about 30 minutes.

Fill half the ice cube tray with cold water and half with the hot water from the kettle.

Place the ice cube tray in the freezer and check every 30 minutes to see if the ice is frozen.

Record how long it takes for the top of the ice in each side of the tray to feel solid.

Once the ice cubes are completely frozen, remove them from the ice cube tray to see if they look different.

MORE FUN
• Use the hot-water technique to make multicolored ice cubes quickly—you can either add food coloring, heat up juice or use colored herbal teas.

LEARNING POINTS
• The phenomenon of hot water freezing faster than cold water is called the Mpemba effect.
• Ice made from tap water looks cloudy because there is air trapped in the water. Boiling the water removes any air dissolved in the water to give clear ice cubes.

SAVE THE RAISINS

Have you ever made a cake or some muffins and found that all the dried fruits or chocolate chips sink to the bottom, giving you a crunchy base you didn't really want? If you sprinkle a little flour over them first they won't sink!

INGREDIENTS

1 cup (125 g) self-rising flour

8 tbsp plus 1 tsp (120 g) unsalted butter, melted

⅔ cup (125 g) superfine (caster) sugar

2 eggs

1 tsp pure vanilla extract

⅓ cup (50 g) raisins or other small dried fruit

4½ tbsp (50 g) chocolate chips

SUPPLIES

Muffin pan

Paper muffin liners

Large bowl

Electric mixer

4 medium bowls

Preheat the oven to 355°F (180°C). Line a 12-cup muffin pan with muffin liners.

In a large bowl, combine the flour, butter, sugar, eggs and vanilla with an electric mixer. Mix until the batter is smooth

Divide the batter into 4 medium bowls. Put plain raisins in the first bowl of batter; raisins coated with flour in the second bowl of batter; plain chocolate chips in the third bowl of batter; and chocolate chips coated in flour in the fourth bowl of batter.

Divide each mixture between 3 paper muffin liners and place the muffin pan in the oven for 15 minutes, or until the cakes are golden brown.

Slice the cakes open. You should find the raisins and chocolate chips coated in flour haven't sunk as much as those not coated in flour.

MORE FUN

- Flour probably won't help with bigger dried fruits (such as candied cherries), but you could give it a go and find out what happens.

LEARNING POINTS

- Dried fruits have a slippery coating of oil on the surface, which makes them sink as the cake rises in the oven. Adding flour helps the fruit grip the cake batter so they don't sink.

- Chocolate chips tend to sink as they are too heavy for the cake mixture to support them. Try using smaller chocolate chips and sprinkle them over the top of the cake just before baking.

Adult Supervision

SUPERHERO-EGG CRESS HEADS

You probably know that plants need sunlight, water, nutrients and the right temperature to grow. But did you know that plants can grow without soil? You can test this out by growing a cress head.

Like humans, plants need water to stay hydrated. Have you ever noticed that a plant low on water starts to droop?

Plants need sunlight for a process called photosynthesis, which requires energy in the form of light to convert carbon dioxide and water to carbohydrates for growth.

Warmer temperatures encourage plants to germinate and grow, while in colder temperatures growth slows down or even stops.

INGREDIENTS
2 eggs
Cress seeds

SUPPLIES
Knife
Egg holder
Markers for decoration
Cotton balls

Boil the eggs until they are hard-boiled, about 6 minutes, and leave them to cool. Carefully slice off the tops of the eggs, remove all the egg whites and yolks and rinse out the shells. Put the shells in the egg holder.

Using markers, decorate your eggshells to look like superheroes.

Dampen a cotton ball and place it inside the eggshell.

Place 10 to 15 cress seeds on the cotton wool and put the superhero egg in a sunny spot.

Once the leaves on the cress turn green, you can eat them.

MORE FUN
- Place plastic cups over the eggshells to act like a greenhouse. Design an investigation to discover whether the cress grows better with or without the greenhouse.

LEARNING POINTS
- Soil contains all the nutrients a plant needs to grow, but it's the nutrients the plant needs, not the soil itself.
- Hydroponics is when plants are grown in water that contains the nutrients it needs rather than soil. Hydroponics is a very useful growing method in areas where there isn't much good soil or where space is limited.

THE PERFECT KETCHUP RACE

Have you ever found ketchup takes too long to drip out of the bottle? This is because it's too thick (viscous) and flows slowly.

Imagine pouring water and syrup down a ramp—the water would flow quickly and the syrup more slowly. This is because water has a low viscosity and syrup, which is thicker, has a higher viscosity.

This activity investigates whether different brands of ketchup have different viscosities.

INGREDIENTS
Different brands of ketchup

SUPPLIES
Small whiteboard, cutting board or wooden plank

Stack of books or a box

Erasable marker

Ruler

Small containers

Stopwatch

Use the whiteboard as a ramp, setting it with a gentle gradient on the stack of books. Draw start and finish lines on the ramp with the erasable marker, using the ruler to ensure the lines are straight.

Add about 5 teaspoons (25 ml) of each brand of ketchup to separate small containers.

Pour the contents of each container down the ramp one by one, starting the stopwatch as they cross the start line and stopping the stopwatch when they cross the finish line.

Is there much difference between the ketchups?

MORE FUN
- Try adding a little vinegar to the slowest ketchup, mixing well, and time how long it takes to flow down the ramp. It should be less viscous after the addition of the vinegar and flow faster.

LEARNING POINTS
- Thicker liquids have a higher viscosity, as they have a lot of internal friction slowing them down as they flow.

finish —

KEEP YOUR FRUIT SALAD COLORFUL

Have you ever made a beautiful fruit salad only to find it turns brown before you have time to serve it? Fruit changes color because oxygen in the air reacts with the surface of the fruit under the skin, making it turn brown.

There are several ways you can preserve the colors of your fruit salad. Adding an acidic juice, such as lemon or lime, stops the chemical reaction happening. Pickling has the same effect, although a pickled fruit salad might not be especially tasty.

One way to keep your fruit salad fresh is to stop oxygen reaching the fruit. This can be done by storing the fruit in water, coating it in a sugar syrup or adding salt.

INGREDIENTS

2 apples, thinly sliced
2 bananas, thinly sliced
Selection of other sliced fruits
1 tsp salt
1 cup (240 ml) water
Fresh or bottled lemon juice
Fresh or bottled lime juice

SUPPLIES

4 small bowls

Divide the apples, bananas and other fruits evenly between 4 small bowls.

Leave the first bowl of fruit plain. This is your control.

Mix the salt with the water and stir until the salt has dissolved. Soak the fruit in the second bowl in the salty water for 5 minutes and then drain the salt water.

Sprinkle the fruit in the third bowl with lemon juice and mix well.

Sprinkle the fruit in the fourth bowl with lime juice and mix well.

Leave all the bowls in the same place and check how they look every 30 minutes.

We wouldn't recommend eating the salty salad!

MORE FUN

- If you cover the top of the fruit salad with one fruit, does this keep the rest fresh?

LEARNING POINTS

- Fruits such as apples are iron-rich so when you cut into them and damage the cells, exposing them to oxygen in the air, a reaction occurs that leads to the formation of iron oxide, which makes the apple look brown. It's a bit like the apple rusting.

 Adult Supervision

EXPLODING CHOCOLATE POPCORN

When you think about it, it's pretty amazing that a tiny kernel of corn can turn into the delicious popcorn treat we know and love.

Popcorn is low-fat, low-calorie and gluten-free, so it's a great healthy snack. For a special occasion, you can add chocolate, butter or another sweet coating.

INGREDIENTS

Oil

Popcorn kernels

Melted dark chocolate

Popping candy

SUPPLIES

Large thick-bottomed pot with lid

Large baking sheet

Parchment paper

Heat the oil in a large, thick-bottomed pot over medium-high heat. Once the oil is hot, add a couple of popcorn kernels and watch them pop. Once they pop, it is hot enough. Carefully add enough popcorn to cover the bottom of the pot.

Place the lid on the pot and wait for the kernels to pop. Gently shake the pan once the popping starts. When the popping slows down, remove the pot from the heat and leave the popcorn to cool.

Cover a large baking sheet with parchment paper and spread the popcorn out on the baking sheet.

Drizzle the melted dark chocolate over the popcorn. Sprinkle popping candy over the chocolate and leave the popcorn in the fridge to set for 5 to 10 minutes.

MORE FUN

- Look at the shape of your popcorn. Does it look like a snowflake or a mushroom? Different types of corn make different shapes of popcorn.

LEARNING POINTS

- Not all types of corn pop. Popcorn has a hull (outer layer) that is just the right thickness to allow it to burst open to reveal a soft starchy middle. Each kernel contains a small drop of water inside. As the popcorn heats up, the water expands and turns into steam. This inflates the starch inside, making it spill out and creating the funny shape we associate with popcorn.

SURPRISE LOLLIPOPS

If you like chocolate, you'll love these surprise chocolate lollipops. The surprise is the flavor, which you get to choose. Then you can ask a friend to guess what you've added. Just go easy with the red pepper flakes!

Remember to be careful as you melt the chocolate, as even a small amount of water can turn your chocolate into a grainy, lumpy mess that won't make a tasty lollipop. Also, overheating can make the chocolate lose its lovely silky texture, so be careful not to overheat it.

INGREDIENTS

Milk chocolate

White chocolate

Dark chocolate

Ground cinnamon

Orange zest

Peppermint extract

Red pepper flakes

Other toppings (fudge, chopped nuts and so on)

SUPPLIES

Large baking sheet

Parchment paper

3 heatproof bowls

Large pot of water

Wooden spoon

Lollipop sticks

Line a large baking sheet with parchment paper.

Melt the milk chocolate, white chocolate and dark chocolate in 3 separate heatproof bowls over a pot of simmering water.

Decide which flavors you want to use—cinnamon, orange zest, peppermint or red pepper flakes—and add a different flavor to each bowl of chocolate.

Carefully pour about 1 tablespoon (15 ml) of one of the melted chocolate mixtures onto the parchment paper and form it into a circle with a wooden spoon. Press a lollipop stick into the chocolate.

Sprinkle the lollipops with toppings and place them in the fridge to set.

MORE FUN

• Try making different shapes of lollipops. Can you make a square, rectangle and oval? How about a star?

LEARNING POINTS

• Chocolate contains cocoa butter, which is high in fat and melts at around body temperature. This is why chocolate is solid at room temperature, but melts easily in your mouth.

Clouds are made up of droplets of water and ice particles floating at different heights. There are lots of different types of clouds whose names are based on their shape and where in the atmosphere they are.

As the sun heats water on the surface of the Earth, it turns into a water vapor, which is a gas. As water vapor rises, it cools and turns back into water, forming a cloud. Clouds float because the droplets of water are very small and light. They float in the atmosphere a bit like you see a speck of dust floating in the air. There is also a constant flow of warm air rising upward beneath the cloud, keeping it afloat. As a cloud grows, the water droplets start to stick to each other and grow bigger and bigger. Eventually they get so big that they are heavy enough to fall downward. This is rain!

In this activity, you can make egg white "clouds" on your breakfast toast to learn about the different types of clouds:

- **Cumulus:** These are big, white, puffy clouds that usually mean good weather.
- **Stratus:** These are flat, low-level clouds that cover a lot of the sky. They often produce a little rain.
- **Cirrocumulus:** These are high clouds that look like cotton balls.
- **Cumulonimbus:** These are very tall clouds that span from low to high. They can cause violent thunderstorms.

Adult Supervision

EGGY CLOUDS

INGREDIENTS

2 eggs
Salt
Pepper
Bread

SUPPLIES

Small baking sheet
Parchment paper
2 small bowls
Electric handheld mixer

MORE FUN

- How many different cloud types can you make?

Preheat the oven to 390°F (200°C).

Line a small baking sheet with parchment paper.

Crack the eggs into a small bowl, reserving the yolks in a separate small bowl. Beat the egg whites, salt and pepper with an electric mixer until you see stiff peaks.

Use the whipped egg whites to create cloud shapes on the parchment paper.

Place the yolks on the baking sheet separate from the egg whites. Bake for about 5 minutes, until the eggs are lightly browned.

Toast a slice of bread and place a cloud and sun yolk on the toast. Sprinkle with additional pepper to make the rain clouds gray.

LEARNING POINTS

- Egg white is about 90 percent water and 10 percent protein. The proteins are long chains of amino acids all tangled up. When you beat egg white, the proteins stretch out and untangle. The whisking introduces bubbles into the mixture, which become trapped between the protein chains to create a foam.

INVENT

This chapter is all about creativity in the kitchen. Invent your own chocolate bar and design packaging to keep it fresh.

Create colorful, healthy gummy sweets and new flavors of marshmallows while learning about the power of gelatin.

Tickle your taste buds with popping candy lollipops and homemade candy powder while keeping your new creations safe in a handspun sugar trap.

This chapter demonstrates sugar science, explores the power of baking powder and uses soda water as a secret ingredient to make the fluffiest of omelets.

Dive in and turn your kitchen into a confectioner's dream.

SUPER SOUR CANDY POWDER

Have you ever wondered why sour candy powder tastes fizzy? Find out why it makes your tongue tickle by making your own. It's much easier than you think.

Bags of this candy powder would make great party favors with some Popping Candy Lollipops (page 146) for some extra fizz!

INGREDIENTS

1 cup (130 g) icing sugar

2 tsp (10 g) food-grade citric acid

1 tsp baking soda

3 drops lemon extract

Lemon or strawberry flavoring

SUPPLIES

Medium bowl

Spoon or whisk

In a medium bowl, combine the icing sugar, citric acid, baking soda, lemon extract and flavoring and mix thoroughly with a spoon.

MORE FUN

- Why not try this with Fruity 3-D Shapes (page 80) or Popping Candy Lollipops (page 146)?
- Try adding a little more lemon extract to make your candy powder extra sour, or try raspberry flavor instead to make it sweet instead of sour.

LEARNING POINTS

- It's the citric acid that makes the candy powder sour. When you put candy powder in your mouth, your saliva makes the citric acid crystals dissolve. These react with the baking soda, producing carbon dioxide gas. It's the carbon dioxide gas that tickles your tongue.

Which flavor will you choose?

What will you dip?

Enjoy the super sour, fizzy flavors.

 Adult Supervision

CRISPY OR CAKEY?

How do you like your cookies? Do you like thin and crispy, thick and gooey or a cross between a cake and a cookie?

This fun investigation shows you which ingredient combination to use to make your cookie just how you like it. Extra flour in a cookie means the mixture spreads out less during baking, giving you a thicker, denser result. The addition of baking soda adds air to the cookie, making it thicker than a cookie with no baking soda and producing a cracked surface.

BASIC COOKIE DOUGH

1 cup minus 1 tsp (225 g) butter, at room temperature

½ cup plus 1 tbsp (110 g) superfine (caster) sugar

2⅛ cups plus 1 tbsp (275 g) all-purpose flour

EXTRA TEST INGREDIENTS

1 tbsp (12 g) baking powder

Chocolate chips

2 tbsp (18 g) all-purpose flour

SUPPLIES

Large baking sheet

Parchment paper

Large bowl

Wooden spoon

4 medium bowls

Preheat the oven to 355°F (180°C). Line a large baking sheet with parchment paper.

To make the basic cookie dough, mix together the butter and sugar in a large bowl with a wooden spoon. Add the flour slowly, until you have a smooth mixture that's a little bit sticky.

Divide the mixture evenly between 4 medium bowls.

Add the baking powder to the first bowl and mix well. Use your hands to mix in a handful of chocolate chips and divide the mixture into 4 evenly sized balls of dough. Place them on the prepared baking sheet and bake for 15 minutes, or until the cookies are lightly brown around the edges.

Add extra flour to the second bowl of dough. Repeat the preceding steps to bake the cookies.

Add only chocolate chips to the dough in the third bowl. Repeat the preceding steps to bake the cookies.

Add chocolate chips to the dough in the fourth bowl. This time, turn the oven up to 390°F (200°C) and bake the cookies for 10 minutes.

MORE FUN

- Try adding chocolate chips and M&M's to the cookie dough. Do you prefer the extra crunch of the M&M's or a smoother chocolate?

LEARNING POINTS

- There are a lot of variables to consider when baking cookies, which is why you need to keep the oven temperature and baking time consistent.
- A low temperature and longer baking time gives you crisper, thinner cookies whereas a higher temperature and shorter baking time will give you softer, thicker cookies.
- Baking powder releases carbon dioxide, which adds air to the cookie mixture. Cookies with baking powder tend to have a soft, fluffy texture.

THE FLUFFIEST EGGS

If you like your eggs light and fluffy, this soda water hack is something you'll use for years to come. A little bit of soda water added to eggs makes them deliciously light and fluffy—and it's all thanks to the bubbles.

INGREDIENTS

3 eggs
2 tbsp (30 ml) soda water
2 tsp (10 g) butter
Omelet toppings

SUPPLIES

Whisk
Small bowl
Small nonstick skillet
Spatula or wooden spoon

Whisk the eggs in a small bowl and slowly add the soda water. Let the mixture sit for a few minutes.

Melt the butter in a small nonstick skillet over medium-high heat until it starts to sizzle. Pour the egg mixture into the skillet and tilt it so the mixture covers the bottom of the skillet. Cook for 2 minutes.

Use the spatula or wooden spoon to gently stir the eggs, so the uncooked eggs run underneath the omelet. Cook for 1 to 2 minutes, until the eggs set. Add your desired toppings, fold the omelet in half and serve.

MORE FUN

- Try replacing half the milk in your usual pancake mixture with soda water. You should find your pancakes are extra fluffy too!
- Does this experiment work as well if your soda water is a little flat?

LEARNING POINTS

- When the egg is heated, the air in the soda water bubbles expands to produce light and airy eggs.

Adult Supervision

GUESS-THE-FLAVOR MARSHMALLOW

Marshmallows make a fun addition to a special hot chocolate and are perfect for a campfire treat as they have a low melting point. But have you ever wondered how they are made?

Originally, marshmallows were made from the sap of the root of the marshmallow plant, but these days gelatin is used instead.

INGREDIENTS

½ tbsp (7 g) powdered gelatin

Water

2½ tbsp (25 g) cornstarch

3 tbsp (25 g) icing sugar

⅘ oz (25 ml) liquid glucose

1 cup plus 3 tbsp (225 g) superfine (caster) sugar

½ tsp flavoring (peppermint extract, lemon extract, orange extract or pure vanilla extract)

SUPPLIES

Large measuring cup

Sieve

Small bowl

Medium pot

Wooden spoon

Candy thermometer (optional)

Electric mixer

Medium baking sheet

Parchment paper

In a large measuring cup, combine the gelatin with ⅓ cup plus 4 teaspoons (100 ml) of cold water. Leave the mixture for 10 minutes to allow the gelatin to absorb the liquid.

Sift the cornstarch and icing sugar into a small bowl with a sieve.

Place the liquid glucose syrup and superfine (caster) sugar in a medium pot over low heat with ½ cup plus 1 teaspoon (125 ml) of water. Heat the mixture slowly, stirring continuously with a wooden spoon, until you have a clear, thick liquid. Reduce the heat to very low and simmer gently for about 15 minutes. If you have a candy thermometer, the temperature should be around 230°F (110°C) at this point, or at the soft-ball stage.

Whisk the gelatin with an electric mixer and carefully add the syrup mixture. Try not to allow the syrup to touch the sides of the whisk.

Once all the syrup has been added, continue to whisk until you get a thick white syrup. Add the flavoring and whisk a bit more.

Line a medium baking sheet with parchment paper and sprinkle half the cornstarch and icing sugar mixture over the parchment paper.

Carefully pour the marshmallow mixture onto the prepared baking sheet and leave the mixture to sit at room temperature for about 2 hours.

Once it is set, cut the marshmallow into squares and dip them in the remaining icing sugar mixture.

(continued)

Adult Supervision

GUESS-THE-FLAVOR MARSHMALLOW (CONT.)

MORE FUN

- Try adding strawberries or raspberries to the marshmallows. Spoon about half the mixture into the prepared baking sheet, then sprinkle icing sugar mixture over the fruit before laying it on top of the marshmallow mixture in the tray. Pour the remaining marshmallow mixture over the fruit and leave to set.

- For an extra special treat, you could melt chocolate to dip the marshmallows in.

LEARNING POINTS

- The melting point of a marshmallow is just above body temperature, which is why they start to change state in your mouth and why they melt so quickly when placed near a fire.

- When the hot sugar syrup is whisked with the gelatin, bubbles form and the gelatin stabilizes the mixture, which is why the marshmallow syrup sets.

 **Adult Supervision**

CHOCOLATE LAB

What's your dream chocolate bar? Do you like the addition of crunch with added nuts, honeycomb or cookies? Or do you prefer a chewier texture with smooth caramel or scrumptious fudge? How about extra sweetness with the addition of fruits or gummy candies? Or some pop and spice with popping candy, ginger or chili?

Set up a chocolate lab and make your very own chocolate bar (and packaging, if desired) with this fun activity.

INGREDIENTS

6¾ oz (200 g) chocolate

Fruity syrups, fudge syrup and caramel syrup (optional)

Toppings (crushed candy canes, nuts, seeds, sprinkles, crushed wafers)

SUPPLIES

Medium heatproof bowl

Large pot of water

Chocolate mold

Break the chocolate into small pieces and place them into a medium heatproof bowl over a pot of simmering water. Heat the chocolate pieces until they have melted.

If you want the chocolate to be flavored, add fruity syrups, fudge syrup or caramel syrup.

Carefully pour the chocolate into the chocolate mold and smooth the top to create an even surface.

Think about the texture and taste you want the top of the chocolate bar to have. For example, melted caramel will give a smooth, rich flavor while nuts, seeds or sprinkles will give a crunchy texture. Sprinkle your toppings over the top and leave the chocolate to cool until it is completely hard.

Carefully remove the chocolate from the mold and test it. Can you taste the flavors you added?

MORE FUN

- Think about how to package your chocolate bar. For it to stay fresh, it needs to be sealed so oxygen in the air can't reach it.

- Design a wrapper using aluminum foil and a plastic bag or paper bag and decorate the wrapper with paper and pens. Don't forget to name your chocolate bar!

LEARNING POINTS

- Remember to heat the chocolate gently. Chocolate is very sensitive to heat and turns lumpy and grainy if heated above 110°F (44°C).

- Don't cover chocolate as you melt it, as moisture can condense on the lid and drip into the chocolate, making it seize. Seizing is when chocolate changes from shiny and smooth to lumpy and grainy.

POPPING CANDY LOLLIPOPS

Lollipops are a lovely sweet treat and very easy to customize at home. You can use molds to make special shapes and add colors and flavors to fit any occasion.

Lollipops are also a great introduction to the science of sugar. This easy recipe shows how sugar needs to be heated to high temperatures to reach the hard-crack stage, which yields a hard lollipop.

INGREDIENTS

2 cups (384 g) sugar
½ cup (120 ml) corn syrup
¼ cup (60 ml) water
Popping candy
Sprinkles and other decorations

SUPPLIES

Large baking sheet
Parchment paper
Medium pot
Wooden spoon
Pastry brush
Candy thermometer
Lollipop sticks

Line a large baking sheet with parchment paper.

Combine the sugar, corn syrup and water in a medium pot over medium heat. Mix well with a wooden spoon and bring the mixture to a boil. Keep stirring until all the sugar has dissolved.

Brush down the sides of the pan with a pastry brush (this stops crystals from forming).

Keep the mixture boiling until a candy thermometer reads 300°F (150°C), or the hard-crack stage. Let the mixture cool for about 5 minutes, then carefully pour the mixture on the prepared baking sheet in circle shapes. Press a lollipop stick into each circle and sprinkle immediately with popping candy, sprinkles and other decorations.

Leave the lollipops to cool and then carefully peel off the parchment paper.

MORE FUN

• If you want to make lollipops but are short on time, you can melt store-bought hard candies in an oven-safe mold. Choose colors and flavors carefully so they blend together well. It'll take only about 5 minutes to melt the candy in the oven.

LEARNING POINTS

• Hard-crack is the hottest stage in candy making and gives a brittle, hard candy. At this temperature, there is almost no water left in the sugar syrup. If you don't have a candy thermometer, drop a little of the hot syrup mixture into cold water and it will form hard, brittle sugar threads that snap when it's at the correct temperature.

• Take care with hot syrup mixtures and allow the sugar threads to cool before taking them out of the cold water.

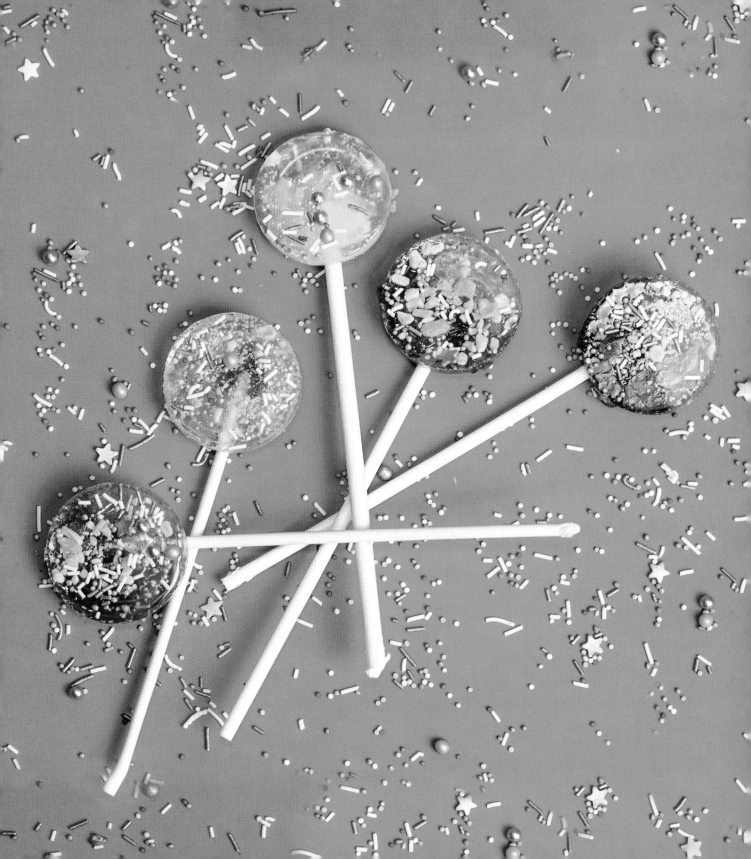

Adult Supervision

FRUITY GUMMY CANDIES

Did you know you can make your own fruity candies? It's super easy! The big advantage of making your own candy is there's no preservatives or food additives and, as you're using fresh juice to make these candies, they are packed with vitamins too.

There's a lot of natural sugar in the fruit juice, so you don't need to add extra sugar and you can make any flavor or shape you want.

INGREDIENTS

6 leaves gelatin

Water

½ cup (120 ml) 100 percent fruit juice

1 tbsp (15 ml) fresh or bottled lemon juice

2 tbsp (30 ml) honey

SUPPLIES

Small bowl

Small baking dish

Parchment paper

Small pot

Wooden spoon

MORE FUN

- Experiment with different flavor combinations. How about apple juice and a little peppermint extract?
- If you have a candy mold, you could use that instead of the baking dish to create more detailed shapes.

Place the gelatin in a small bowl and cover it with a layer of water. Leave the gelatin for 5 to 10 minutes.

Line a small baking dish with parchment paper.

Place the fruit juice, lemon juice and honey in a small pot over medium heat and bring the mixture to a boil. Reduce the heat to low.

Squeeze any excess moisture out of the gelatin leaves and place them in the juice mixture until they dissolve.

Stir the mixture well with a wooden spoon. Pour it into the prepared baking dish and refrigerate it overnight.

Once the gelatin is set, cut it into small pieces.

LEARNING POINTS

- Gelatin is a processed form of collagen, which is the most common protein found in humans and other mammals.
- When the gelatin is dissolved in hot water, the bonds holding the collagen proteins together are broken. As the gelatin cools new bonds form, trapping the juice and other ingredients in the candy.
- Gelatin is also used to make Jell-O. Jell-O wobbles as there's so much water trapped between the gelatin bonds, but since candy has less liquid than Jell-O it is more solid.
- Did you know the word "collagen" comes from the Greek word "kolla," which means "glue"?

SUGAR TRAP

Spun sugar makes a super fancy decoration with which to top cakes and desserts. It might look tricky to make, but it's actually very simple.

This activity makes a sugar trap. What will you trap in the cooled sugar and how many different shapes can you make?

INGREDIENTS

Superfine (caster) sugar

SUPPLIES

Bowl

Oil

Medium pot

Whisk or wooden spoon

Cover a glass bowl with a thin layer of oil and place the bowl upside down.

Gently heat the sugar in a medium pot over medium heat until it has dissolved. Let the sugar come to a boil, without stirring, until it turns a caramel color and is thick enough to drip off a spoon in strands.

Remove the sugar from the heat and use a whisk or wooden spoon to drizzle it over the upside-down bowl. Be careful, as the sugar will be very hot.

Leave the sugar to set and remove it from the bowl. You now have a sugar trap. If you can't remove the sugar cage easily, place the bowl in the fridge for 5 to 10 minutes and the sugar trap should pop off easily.

MORE FUN

- Add a little food coloring and flavoring to the sugar mixture once you remove it from the heat. Dip the whisk into the mixture and lift out of the pan so strings of melted sugar hang down. Carefully wrap the sugar strands around a lollipop stick. When the sugar is cool enough to touch, mold it with your hands into a lollipop shape.

LEARNING POINTS

- When sugar melts, it caramelizes. This is when molecules of sucrose (granulated sugar) break down into glucose and fructose and then break down further into carbon, hydrogen and oxygen, which react with one another to form new compounds that give the flavor and smell of caramelized sugar.

ACKNOWLEDGMENTS

As always, I need to thank my incredibly patient husband, who encourages and supports me in everything I do by taking care of the kids, brainstorming ideas and helping out with my late-night creating.

Thanks to my friends for cheering me on when things get tricky and being the most invaluable support network.

My children inspire and motivate me daily with their creativity and endless questioning. They have been involved with every activity in this book: thinking of ideas, testing recipes and, of course, giving their verdict on the final product. *Snackable Science Experiments* has very much been a family creation with much valued input from even the littlest member.

A huge thank-you to Charlotte for not only taking amazing photographs but also for working long days to get the shots we needed, washing up late at night and vacuuming the layer of sugar and flour that collected over most of the house.

Thanks also to the lovely Page Street Publishing team for inspiring me to write a second book and once again guiding me through the process so expertly.

ABOUT THE AUTHOR

Emma is a professional science blogger following her dream of making science fun for even the youngest of children.

She has been creating exciting and easy science investigations for Science Sparks since 2011 and can't think of anything she would rather be doing.

Emma is mum to four children whose endless questioning and creativity inspire many of her ideas.

INDEX